RADICAL GROWTH

A GUIDEBOOK TO GROWING A VIBRANT LIFE

HAVILAH CUNNINGTON

Cover Design & Layout by Hans Bennewitz (modedesign.us)

Special Thanks to Soo Prince for your amazing efforts on this project!

AUTHOR'S STORY

I love the word vibrant. Maybe because it means full of energy and enthusiasm. And let's be honest... *Who doesn't want a life like this?* It's not easy to live in this world, so the thought of a vibrant life is rather appealing. If most of us hung our lives out on the clothesline we would see lives full of things to do but not always full of energy and enthusiasm... *I know I did.*

Many years ago, I found myself in a place of complete and utter devastation. I was a new mother of two and the thought of taking care of these little boys every day was not only overwhelming, but completely excruciating. I happened to walk into my pediatrician's office one day believing it was just a simple visit. You know, the "walk-in, walk-out" kind of appointment. I was shocked to discover that that day was about to change my entire life. It's the very reason you're holding this book in your hands right now. It was a game-changing day.

The pediatrician didn't say much, but when I explained how overwhelmed I was, she said, *"You don't seem like the type of woman to be as overwhelmed as you are."* As soon as she spoke that phrase, tears welled up in my eyes and my vision of her began to blur into a messy silhouette. She then said these defining words, *"I think you have postpartum depression."* When she said it, my heart jumped forward as if it wanted to grab the words right out of her hands. *"That's it!"* I thought. All of the shame-filled months and weary routine suddenly looked different. I had found hope. *"I wasn't crazy!"*

Depression has a way of isolating you. And let's be honest, my pastoral position and teaching platform didn't help matters. I simply allowed the waves of shame and condemnation to fill my everyday life. I just needed to pray more, I was sure of it. I just needed a vacation, a spa treatment or... well someone to take my family for a couple of days... or weeks. I just needed to get my head clear. Never mind my exhausted body and the demands of my newborn baby, I was a mess. This diagnosis was the very thing I needed. A simple and profound validation. This pediatrician, unbeknownst to her, was the truth bringer and radical shifter that I needed. I clumsily got into my car, placing both babies in their seats. I can still picture the drive home on that rainy day. As I drove, I remembered a conversation with a friend who, in passing, had mentioned that her mother was a Christian counselor. I fumbled my phone, dialing the number as fast as I could, almost believing that if I didn't do it now, I might never have the courage to do it.

I left a very simple message. *"Hello, my name is Havilah and I need help. My doctor thinks I might have postpartum depression and I need to see someone. Please call me back."* It wasn't much more than a day later and I was walking into her office, meeting a woman that I would spend nearly two years with, seeing her almost every week.

She began by asking me a series of questions to see if I might have the basic symptoms of postpartum. When we were done she said, *"Well, you have 12 of the 13 symptoms."* I was a mess! I sheepishly asked her, *"What do I need to do?"* because remember, I'm a pastor, I'm a leader, I'm a catalyst. Leaders like to do things. She confidently said, *"I want you to get three full nights of sleep, and once you're rested we will talk."* That was it?! I could feel relief running down me like cool rain on a hot day. It was music to my ears, medication to my wounds. So I did just that. I went home and explained to my husband,

Ben, that I needed to work on one thing and one thing only... SLEEP!

As days turned into weeks and weeks turned into months, those months eventually turned into years and my life began to radically shift towards growth.

There wasn't a specific moment where everything shifted; it was more like continual little shifts that turned into bigger shifts. I was changing and growing like the expanding belly of a pregnant woman! My hunger for life and God was returning. My thoughts were changing and slowly I was being transformed. The process was working!

It was my counselor who looked at me one day and told me something I hadn't considered before. She said, *"You would have eventually ended up in my office because you were headed towards an emotional and physical crash. The pregnancy just got you here sooner."*

It's funny how life turns out. At the age of seventeen and a half I gave my life to Christ in a wholehearted moment, and by the grace of God, I have never looked back. I've never regretted one moment serving God and giving Him my life. It's been such an honor to serve Him and be used by Him to touch peoples' lives, but like that famous quote says, *"God doesn't have to abuse you, to use you."* This would have been written on my tombstone. To be specific, during one season of my early life in Christ, I remember being diagnosed with ulcers at age 23. At that time I was working an 80 hour week with very little time given to a 'Sabbath.'

One of the hardest parts about ministry, or any other role in life that we immensely enjoy, is that our internal parameters are hard to find. Because it's enjoyable to work hard and experience results, it can be difficult to know when it's time to clock in and clock out. But, like anything, we need to have a day of rest. If God needed a day of rest then certainly we do also.

So this is where I got to work. Finding ways to create Godly boundaries and protect what I liked to call "My Yard." I learned what it was that God held me responsible for and what He took care of. I learned that as I took care of myself and stewarded what was mine to steward, I could serve others out of the overflow. Only when my little world was healthy and safe was I truly going to have a vibrant fruitful life that would benefit others!

INTRODUCTION
So You Want A Vibrant Life?

Bible Gateway describes a VIBRANT life as follows:

"In John 15, at a time when all of His disciples are feeling as if they are about to be uprooted, Jesus sketches a picture of this new life as a flourishing vineyard—a labyrinth of vines and strong branches steeped in rich soil, abundant grapes hanging from their vines ripening in the sun. Jesus sculpts a new Garden of Eden in their imaginations—one that is bustling with fruit, sustenance, and satisfying aromas. This is the Kingdom life. It is all about connection, sustenance, and beauty."

How many of us want our lives to look and feel like this? "Flourishing" with "strong branches" and "abundant grapes"? This is the life that Jesus described. A life with deep roots in Him, able to thrive in every season.

Let's be honest! No one has a vibrant life on accident. No one has a flourishing garden unintentionally. We know God tells us that in order to be fruitful, we must be connected to and abiding in Him (the vine), allowing the Father (the Gardener) to prune and tend us.

So, what does vibrant living look like on a daily basis? Especially when we are busy people, often with precious little time to ourselves.

Vibrant living looks like a life grown on purpose. It's living in such a way that shows we understand what God intended. It's having the Abundant life He promised. It's not some fantasy, unattainable, and envy-provoking vision or a dream that torments us with its impossibility. It's a life that's within our reach!

Vibrant living is possible, but we have to submit to the process. We have to trust the Gardener.

Before we begin, I want you to understand a few things about The Laws of Growth:

1. **All growth starts at baseline.** None of us have been born fully formed and ready to go. We can learn from others' experience or our own but eventually we have to try it out ourselves. Everyone starts out as a beginner. So relax… *You'll get there!*

2. **Growth happens slowly.** There is no such thing as overnight success in the Kingdom; only incremental growth. No matter how gifted, privileged, or talented you might be, growth is a gradual process. One person might look like they are growing faster than you. *Don't be tempted to compare…* growth is measured in years rather than moments.

3. **Certain conditions and particular environments are necessary for growth.** When a baby is born, it requires particular care for that stage of its development. If you don't care for the infant properly, it will not thrive. It's important to understand that not all environments and conditions lend themselves to growth. There are, and will be, environments and seasons that are perfect for your growth. Sometimes you will have to intentionally find them.

4. **Growth can be traced through "Stages of Development."** Each stage is vital and cannot be skipped. They are predictable and normative phases to spiritual growth. Don't worry, all mature Christians have passed through these stages. It's important to have grace for yourself and for others who may be working their way through them. *It's not always pretty!*

5. **Progressing through all stages of development can only be considered successful growth.** There are NO short cuts when it comes to full maturity. We may make it to our promised land sooner than 40 years but we all have to walk through the desert. Maturity isn't a gift... it's a process. Have faith. *You may not be where you want to be but... You're on your way!*

I have written this simple Guidebook to help you increase your capacity to be fruitful and flourish. I have kept it simple because most people have busy lives, so it means you can take each day in bite-size chunks. Its simplicity will help you focus on one thing at a time, enabling you to enjoy the journey of watching your life flourish and become vibrant!

This is written to be a daily devotional, but don't worry if you don't do the days consecutively, or if you can't get to it every day; instead just commit to finish the days when you can.

HOW IT WORKS

Each week, I will introduce you to the 'theme' for the week and give you a picture of where we're headed and what we're going to cover. Each day, we will start with a few short paragraphs introducing the day, followed by three smaller sections as follows:

 MORNING MEDITATION

In this section, I will give you a scripture or thought to meditate on. The word meditate means to *"think deeply and carefully about something or to focus one's mind for a period of time; to ponder, muse and reflect; mull over or chew on."* Wow, well, there's a challenge right there! Once you have pondered for a while I may give you a question or two to think on and answer.

 **DAYTIME DARE**

There's a famous quote that says, *"If you do what you've always done, then you'll get what you've always got."* Meaning that, if we want growth, we may need to change our thoughts and/or our behavior. The object of this part of the book is to help you challenge yourself to do something different or something you might normally be scared to do. **This is a small exercise for you to do during the day, based on the morning meditation.** If the challenge that's set doesn't fit with what you received from the meditation, then set your own 'dare.' Either way, make sure you are a taking a dare into the day with you!

 EVENING REFLECTION

This is a time to reflect on the day. It is really important to celebrate yourself! Even if you feel like you may have 'failed'; celebrate that you tried. It means there is progress and you are moving forward! Thankfulness waters the soil of our hearts and keeps it soft and rich.

WEEK 1
Baseline

UNDERSTANDING THE BASICS
"A good life is a fruit-bearing tree."
Proverbs 11:30 (MSG)

Our fruitfulness is in the heart of God. From the very outset of creation, He commanded we be fruitful. Yes, He wants us to multiply physically and reproduce mankind, but He also wants us to multiply and increase the spiritual and emotional fruit in our lives, too.

Throughout the Old Testament, whenever God spoke of fruitfulness, it equated with His favor, with prosperity and the rewards of labor. The picture of being fruitful is used throughout the Bible to illustrate a successful life and to describe the Promised Land. Even Jesus is described in Isaiah 11:1 as *"...the branch from Jesse springing forth that will bear fruit."*

In the Book of Matthew, Jesus said we will be known by our fruit. *Wow... that's pretty clear!*

The theme for this coming week is 'BASELINE: Understanding the Basics.' Remember the first Law of Growth is *All of growth starts at baseline.* None of us have been born fully formed and ready to go. We can learn from others' experience or try it out ourselves. Everyone starts out as a beginner. *So relax... You'll get there!*

First we are going to look at a part of the process to becoming fruitful and then we will look at our make-up; i.e., that we are triune beings made up of body, soul and spirit.

Everyone originates with the same seed. Everyone is given the same exact sun and we all have been placed here by the same Gardener. How we prepare our soil and tend our garden is the number one factor affecting our growth. Don't worry... everyone starts small. You may feel like you don't have much, but you have enough... *And I'm going to show you how to grow those mustard seeds!*

DAY 1 : *Becoming Fruitful*

We were made to bear fruit and to come into the 'fullness' of life that Jesus promised. We were made to have a 'garden' teeming with life and full of abundant fruit. So if we don't bear fruit, we struggle with boredom, with the mundanity of life and can feel hopeless. You can be busy without being fruitful! *It's true!* But if you are not fruitful, you won't be fulfilled.

Fruit is a sign of freedom.

Growing fruit requires us to trust the heart of God; that what He says about how we go about life will set us up for success. So becoming fruitful brings a deep sense of confidence and trust in God!

It's an exciting thing when you start bearing fruit in areas where you haven't previously. Ask God to help you. Don't prop yourself up, you were not meant to do this alone. He *wants* you to be fruitful and enjoying abundance!

 MORNING MEDITATION

In Psalm 1:1–3 in the Amplified it says: "Blessed (happy, fortunate, prosperous, and enviable) is the man whose... delight and desire are in the law of the Lord.... he shall be like a tree firmly planted and tended by the streams of water, ready to bring forth its fruit in its season; its leaf also shall not fade or wither; and everything he does shall prosper and come to maturity."

*What is God saying here and promising you? Take a moment
to ask yourself and your heart: "Do I feel happy, fortunate
and prosperous?"*

Having your roots in god - he will take
care of you so that you can flourish
and provide for others. I do, but
not as strongly rooted in that
as I should be.

*Is your delight and desire still for Him or has it faded?
Journal your thoughts here:*

Fades at time but is strong right
now as I am growing. Have
more desire for him than
true delight.

 DAYTIME DARE

The word "delight" in the original Hebrew means, "to
take pleasure in." The dictionary says it means, "to please
someone greatly."

God wants you to be fruitful and vibrant! In this verse, He is
letting you know that if you continually delight in Him then
you will be so fruitful that it will be enviable to others when
they look at your life.

As you go about your day, pause the constant chatter in your
head and take a moment to deliberately tell Him what you
love about Him; what it is about Him that brings you such
delight. Rekindle the flame of love by using your words and
the attitude of your heart to thank Him. If you can, commit to
doing this more than once during the day.

E **EVENING REFLECTION**

So how was today? Did you manage to have those 'moments of delight?' Journal any internal changes that you felt. Pay attention to what happened in your heart, your emotions and your sense of connection with Him.

Focusing on all he has/is doing for me brings me delight and thankfulness. It was a hard day but I can feel him promising to take care of me.

The original Hebrew word also means "desire; longing." As you reflect on the day, tell Him about the longing you have for more of Him; for more fruitfulness in Your life. Thank Him that He's faithful to do what He promised.

> *"The two most important days in your life are the day you're born and the day you find out why."*
> — *Mark Twain*

Why did God create you? The easiest answer is found in the first chapter of the Bible. Genesis explains that we were made in God's image and our purpose is to contain Him.

"For what purpose did God create man? Only that man might be His container...It is clearly seen in Romans 9:21, 23 and 2 Corinthians 4:7, that God created us to be His containers. We are only empty containers, and God intends to be our only content." — The Economy of God by Witness Lee.

So, when it comes to how we were made, it is fundamental that we understand two things: we were made *by* God and *for* God. I love Mike Bickle's quote that says, *"I am loved (by God) and I am a lover (of God), therefore I am successful."*

Let's look at this a little deeper. If, according to Witness Lee in the first quote, we are containers, how and where do we contain God? Well, let's start with how the Bible says we are formed. In 1 Thessalonians 5:23 it says that we are triune beings, i.e., containing three parts; a spirit, a soul (made up of your mind, will and emotions) and a body.

"Now may the God of peace make you holy in every way, and may your whole spirit and soul and body be kept blameless until our Lord Jesus Christ comes again." (NLT)

Therefore, if God is making us "holy in every way," all three parts have the ability to contain God and be filled by Him.

Having been filled by Him, then out of the overflow we cannot help but express who He is to those around us through each of those parts. You are a spiritual being and just like a hand fits inside a glove, so God's Spirit fits inside your spirit. Your spirit was made to fully contain God!

The Bible says that each of us has a spirit and that spirit was dead until Christ came. Picture your spirit like a deflated balloon when it was dead to God. Then when you were "made alive" in Christ (1 Peter 3:18) the 'balloon' got filled with God's Spirit and your spirit inflated with Him and became BIG inside of you. Your spirit communicates with God because Spirit talks to spirit. Your 'alive' spirit gives you the ability to hear His voice and understand His thoughts.

Galatians 4:6–7 says, *"You can tell for sure that you are now fully adopted as his own children because God sent the Spirit of his Son into our lives crying out, "Papa! Father!" Doesn't that privilege of intimate conversation with God make it plain that you are not a slave, but a child?"* (MSG)

(M) MORNING MEDITATION

"The Spirit, not content to flit around on the surface, dives into the depths of God, and brings out what God planned all along. Who ever knows what you're thinking and planning except you yourself? The same with God—except that he not only knows what he's thinking, but he lets us in on it."
1 Corinthians 2:10–11 (MSG)

Meditate on this. Ponder the wonder of the powerful flow between you and God that is described here; you knowing yourself and your thoughts, the Holy Spirit knowing your thoughts and God's thoughts, and the depths of God that He "dives into" to reveal things to you so that you get to know how He thinks... *wow!*

 **DAYTIME DARE**

Re-read Mike Bickle's quote, *"I am loved (by God) and I am a lover (of God), therefore I am successful,"* and take it into your day as a declaration. At every point you start becoming aware that your circumstances start to dictate your feelings and your feelings want to rule the day, declare this over yourself. In this way you are training your spirit to be the one that governs your soul and not the other way around.

 **EVENING**

Reflect on your day. John 6:63 says, *"The Spirit gives life; the flesh counts for nothing. The words I have spoken to you – they are full of the Spirit and life."* Did you manage to speak words of life over yourself today?

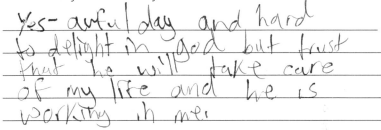

Yes - awful day and hard to delight in god but trust that he will take care of my life and he is working in me.

*"You will receive power when the Holy Spirit
comes on you; and you will be my witness…
to the ends of the earth."*
Acts 1:8 (NIV)

The Holy Spirit is God's presence within us. He is part of the Trinity (the Father, the Son, and the Holy Spirit). Obviously, He is supernatural, He is all-powerful, He knows everything, and He is not limited by time and space.

As we learned yesterday, you are a spiritual being. There is a God-shaped hole in each of us until the Holy Spirit comes and fills it. God's Spirit, when invited in to our lives, enables us to "live and move and have our being" in Him (Acts 17:28 [NIV]). So when it comes to vibrant living, the Holy Spirit in you brings that vibrancy and that abundance from heaven, to your heart and life. This is not just for life on this earth alone, but for all eternity. We know this because of what 2 Corinthians 1:22 says.

"He anointed us, set his seal of ownership on us, and put His Spirit in our hearts as a deposit, guaranteeing what is to come." (NIV)

Once you invite His Spirit to live in you, you begin living in eternity, starting from now, and when you die your spirit will simply transition out of your physical body, from earth to heaven.

In John 14:26, Jesus says that The Holy Spirit was sent to "act on His behalf" and in His place. Instead of having a God walking beside us in the flesh, we now have God living within us.

This verse promises that from within us, the Holy Spirit will comfort us when we're hurting, bring us peace, strengthen us, intercede for us, counsel us, and help us recall the things we've learned and read about God.

"But the Comforter (Counselor, Helper, Intercessor, Advocate, Strengthener, Standby), the Holy Spirit, whom the Father will send in My name [in My place, to represent Me and act on My behalf], He will teach you all things. And He will cause you to recall (will remind you of, bring to your remembrance) everything I have told you." (AMP)

What an incredible gift to us He is! He lives in constant connection and relationship with God, He is full of life and joy and vibrancy, and because He knows all about God, He is always seeking to make Him and His ways known to us.

"But when he, the Spirit of truth, comes, he will guide you into all the truth. He will not speak on his own; he will speak only what he hears, and he will tell you what is yet to come. He will glorify me because it is from me that he will receive what he will make known to you." John 16:13–14 (NIV)

(M) MORNING MEDITATION

We read in Ephesians 5:18, "Don't be drunk with wine, because that will ruin your life. Instead, be filled with the Holy Spirit" (NLT).

The words "be filled" are a command from God. This scripture says 'don't rely on' synthetic things like alcohol, drugs, TV or anything else we might use to find satisfaction. Rather, be filled with the Holy Spirit, because He will authentically fill our life with power and contentment.

Pause for a moment with God. Meditate on the fact that you have authentic power available to you at any given moment of the day because the Holy Spirit fills you. Invite Him to show you anything that you rely on instead of Him.

Jesse, Sleep, TV, wine/beer, food, attention, school-good grades, makeup, clothes, music

 DAYTIME DARE

When we depend on our personal strength to live our Christian life we're shutting out the Holy Spirit, and Paul calls this very unwise. *"Are you so foolish? After beginning with the Spirit, are you now trying to attain your goal by human effort?"* *Galatians 3:3* (NIV)

The results of ignoring the Spirit and His help, and living life on our own, are painful; worry, bad attitudes, habits that are destructive, lust, rebellion, jealousy, unhealthy relationships. We each have our own list.

He wants us to be honest about our need. Tell Him you are sorry for anything that was revealed to you in the meditation and for trying to do life in your own strength. Ask Him to fill you right now. Commit to ask Him at every moment during today to help you.

E EVENING REFLECTION

Reflect on your day. Did you notice how different it was when you invited the Holy Spirit to help you with situations, conversations or circumstances? Celebrate this new partnership you are creating with Him. Feel His delight and pleasure over you as you do.

Its a relief when he takes over and my trust is on him. Still hard not to control things and to always acknowledge him but when I do its great.

"You don't have a soul. You are a soul. You have a body."
— *C.S. Lewis*

Today, we are going to look at your soul and it's function in your life.

In Genesis 2:7 it says that Man was created as a *"living soul."* Your soul is made up of your mind, your will and your emotions. This is very different from your spirit. Your soul is the place where regeneration takes place. Here's what I mean…

When Christ comes to live inside of you, Your spirit becomes "born-again" at once. It doesn't need to be regenerated because it is brand new and works perfectly. The Bible tells you are a new creation. Romans 6:7–11 says that you are no longer bound by sin or enslaved to it, but have an ability to live a life free from sin and all the destruction and devastation that comes with it.

"For when we died with Christ we were set free from the power of sin… We are sure of this because Christ was raised from the dead, and he will never die again… When he died, he died once to break the power of sin… So you also should consider yourselves to be dead to the power of sin." (NLT)

Your mind, your will and your emotions (your soul), on the other hand, must be transformed. How do we know this? Romans 12:2 encourages us to be transformed by a renewing process: *"…let God transform you into a new person by changing the way you think."* (NLT)

Or even better, The Message translates it as *"...fix your attention on God. You'll be changed from the inside out. Readily recognize what he wants from you, and quickly respond to it."*

In 2 Corinthians 10:5–6 it clarifies that the kind of renewal we are called to is from the inside out. It says that it involves casting down arguments and getting rid of wrong thoughts that keep us from God; setting our thoughts on Him and keeping them there. *"We use our powerful God-tools for ... fitting every loose thought and emotion and impulse into the structure of life shaped by Christ. Our tools are ready at hand for clearing the ground of every obstruction and building lives of obedience into maturity."* (MSG)

I like to say, "Your mind has a mind of its own." This is where most Christians get discouraged. They think that what they have been given is not working. They believe their struggle is with the behavior of sinning but really it's with the process of renewal.

The writer of Proverbs puts it like this: *"Above all else, guard your heart, for everything you do flows from it."* Proverbs 4:23 (NIV)

We see here that the "heart" is central to our lives and is the seat of our emotions and will. Simply put, our emotions and our will must be renewed as well as our mind.

"A natural (soulish) man does not accept the things of the Spirit of God, for they are foolishness to him; and he cannot understand them, because they are spiritually appraised (discerned only through the Spirit.)" 1 Corinthians 2:14 (NASB)

If our soul is not renewed and brought under the governing of our spirit-man then we will not be able to discern what God is doing in our lives.

(M) MORNING MEDITATION

"Toxic thoughts in your mind will poison your spirit and your soul." —Beni Johnson.

God loves us! He is fully aware that we are called to love, nurture and share our hearts, and we do well at this. However, it can be challenging for us to keep our emotions or our emotional state from being the thing that is in charge of our day or our lives! Meditate on Philippians 4:8.

"Summing it all up, friends, I'd say you'll do best by filling your minds and meditating on things true, noble, reputable, authentic, compelling, gracious—the best, not the worst; the beautiful, not the ugly; things to praise, not things to curse." (MSG)

Focusing on God and his truths, what he has made for me, given me, what he has for me, Not the world, and the evil and lies but only on the truth of god

DAYTIME DARE

Yesterday you got to practice inviting the Holy Spirit to help and empower you as you went about your day. Today, concentrate specifically on asking Him for help when your emotions are all over the place. Notice that there is a connection between what you think and how you feel and bring to mind Philippians 4:8.

E EVENING REFLECTION

How was today? Journal what went on. Even if you only got
as far as just being aware that your emotions are all over
the place quite often (or more often than you thought,) that's
progress! Celebrate with the Holy Spirit that you have an
adventure ahead of you in exploring the full depths and
capacity of His ability to help and empower you.

I really let god dictate
over my feelings. Dwelled
on his presence all day.
Still need to be able to
be aware of his voice but
I delighed in him most of the
day.

DAY 5 : *Your Body*

"The physical part of you is not some piece of property belonging to the spiritual part of you. God owns the whole works. So let people see God in and through your body."
1 Corinthians 6:19 (MSG)

We have learned that the Holy Spirit inhabits our spirit. Well, God also says that the body He gave you is a place where He dwells. It's a temple! The NIV translates the above scripture like this.

"Do you not know that your bodies are temples of the Holy Spirit, who is in you, whom you have received from God? You are not your own; you were bought at a price. Therefore honor God with your bodies."

It's important to understand that your body, your soul and your spirit all contain the Spirit of God. He gets to inhabit the whole of you! It's also important to realize how intrinsically each part is linked and connected to the others. Therefore, it is impossible to do something with your body that doesn't touch and have an effect on your soul and spirit.

When it comes to living a VIBRANT life, which Ephesians 1:4 tells us we have been called to, we must understand this includes our whole being. Your body is valuable to God because it houses Him and therefore the way you care for and protect it matters to God. He views your body as a place of holiness.

I love the verse in the Bible that talks about being an athlete.

"So I run with purpose in every step. I am not just shadowboxing. I discipline my body like an athlete, training it to do what it should. Otherwise, I fear that after preaching to others I myself might be disqualified." 1 Corinthians 9:26–27 (NLT)

What Paul is describing is one of his core values. That *he* leads his body; not the other way round. We have to renew our heart, our mind and our will. We have to discipline our body. Paul disciplines his body because he knows it has the potential for leading him astray. He is in charge of his body and in this scripture it's clear that this is not up for debate! He will not allow his body to disqualify him.

I have small children around the house. At least a few times a week you will hear me say, "I am the boss of you!" I say it jokingly, of course, but it gets the message across. It basically says, "I'm in charge, in case you are wondering!" This is basically what Paul is saying to himself and then he is explaining his internal narrative in order to benefit us. It sounds like, "Body, I tell you what you can and cannot do. You are not in charge. I am the boss of you."

 MORNING MEDITATION

Many times our body will dominate our world when our soul and spirit needs are not being taken care of. Is your body dominating your life? Is your physical state or condition affecting your ability to connect spiritually with God? Does your body come first and is it ruling your mind, will and emotions? Take a moment and surrender your physical frame to God.

Ask Him to convict you when your need for physical comfort dominates your life rather than your spirit.

any touch is craved, as I get stronger temptation lessens, don't need physical touch, keep body healthy

 **DAYTIME DARE**

A peaceful heart leads to healthy body. Proverbs 14:30 (NIV) says, *"Envy rots the bones!"* Take a moment in your day when you feel physical discomfort and ask yourself is your heart hurting your body? Is jealousy (for example) contaminating your life? Is your physical discomfort connected to a depressed soul?

holding onto Jesse, holding on to the comfort, long for the intimacy but need to find my intimacy with god, and be fully satisfied with him

EVENING REFLECTION

This week, we learned how to become fruitful! True life comes from our spirit. When our spirit talks to God, our spiritual life begins to grow. We learned the Holy Spirit gives us what we need to grow a VIBRANT life. We explored how our soul must be renewed and that that is our responsibility. We also looked at bringing our physical body under the submission of the Holy Spirit and our spirit.

Reflect on the week. Thank God that these new truths are part of your spiritual journey. Thank Him that He knew what He was doing when He created you!

He is working in me. I need to believe that he is right there and be, aware of him. He is great and has taken care of me and will continue to, He is all I need - I need to believe that

You're holy, hes here, ask, Search be ~~quite~~ alert, and have no fear

WEEK 2
Growth

THE SLOW PROCESS

"Oh, the joys of those who do not follow the advice of the wicked, or stand around with sinners, or join in with mockers. But they delight in the law of the Lord, meditating on it day and night. They are like trees planted along the riverbank, bearing fruit each season. Their leaves never wither, and they prosper in all they do."
Psalm 1:1–3 (NLT)

So, how do we grow? The Bible has a lot of parables from nature that are significant and powerful. Like the one above from Psalm 1. This kind of imagery is so helpful for us because it gives us a picture of how growth comes about in our lives. So when it says, "like trees planted along the riverbank, bearing fruit each season," we see a vivid picture in our minds of our lives being a tree like that. I know I did, and I thought; *"Wow, what would it be like to live a life where I would never feel like I was in a drought; where I would feel continually refreshed and able to draw water at any time? What do I have to do?"* So I looked up the rest of the passage and it told me how. It required me to make choices about the influences I allowed in my life; and who I went to for advice. It showed me that my source of water and refreshment represented my diligence in continually sowing the Word of God into my life.

God is the great Gardener of our lives. A gardener studies his ground, the possible products and available seed. He seeks to get rid of the weeds, briers and poisonous plants, in order that the seed He plants has good conditions to grow his fruit to perfection. So the ground of our hearts and characters must be purged from the weeds and things that hinder our growth and we must allow the Gardener to prune our growth with great love and affection. But remembering that in everything He does, He is after growth, enlargement, and productiveness.

Growth happens slowly. There is no such thing as overnight success in the Kingdom; only incremental growth. No matter how gifted, privileged, or talented, you might be, growth is a gradual process. One person might look like they are growing faster than you. *Don't be tempted to compare...* growth is measured in years rather than moments.

If we go back to the image of the tree in Psalm 1, we see that a tree needs growth in the roots in order to be secure and bear fruit. The roots of a tree must go deeper and deeper still, so as to get a really good grip on the earth below, because that's where it gets its support. Without this the tree will fall over when it gets top-heavy or it will be uprooted and blown over in a strong storm. So, in an individual's heart and character, there must be a deepening process happening beneath the surface.

This really means growth in secret, growth out of sight, and being on our own with Him. Again, this book comes out of those months and years that I was growing out of sight and will hopefully help you to grow as you journey this with me!

*"In God's garden of grace, even a broken tree
can bear fruit."*
— *Rick Warren*

God was the very first gardener! In the beginning, we find that He loved to create and watch things grow. God's nature is built around growth; He can't help Himself, it's just who He is! As a Creator, His very nature is to plant for the purpose of growth. Our ability to surrender to God as the chief Gardener of our hearts and lives is vital to our personal development.

Like the plants of the earth, our purpose is to grow, mature and produce fruit at the hands of the Master Gardener. He nurtures us with the light of knowledge and the water of love, giving us all we need if we want it. God is a Gardener at the highest level. He is a Master at what He does. The incredible thing is that He doesn't just tend to the garden of our lives, He provides the environment and the elements that help us to be fruitful. He is not only the Gardener, but He is the Sun — the power that gives us the energy to grow and mature.

My Mom loves to garden! As an aspiring gardener, I find myself asking for all kinds of advice. "Where should I plant this? Does this grow here? Can I plant these together?" She graciously answers all my questions, explaining the different environments that plants need; things I hadn't ever thought about. Like, I didn't know that the sun burns some plants or that others needed to be "soaked" at the roots. It's like a whole new world!

Just like my Mom, God is the Master Gardener. He is very intentional. He never plants things without thinking about the environment He is planting in, the conditions that will affect growth and the fruit that He wants to see at the end. God is a God of purpose, and not passive or inactive. He 'rolls His sleeves up' and gets to work with us and on us. He doesn't stand off to the side like a spectator, over in the shadows. He is right there in the middle of our lives.

As Paul says, He is 'working in all things' (1 Corinthians 12:6) continually and specifically. He is not purposeless. He cannot look at things 'without form, and empty' and not do something. He wants to see change, growth, development and fruitfulness! He wants to plant and create and He is lavish with it. That's why He never ceases to pursue us and woo us. It's why He convicts and prunes us, because He sees the fruit that He has already planned for us to produce and He is committed to seeing VIBRANT growth in our lives.

(M) MORNING MEDITATION

God is an intentional Gardener, so what does He look for from us?

John 15:4 says, *"Abide in Me, and I will abide in you. A branch cannot bear fruit if it is disconnected from the vine, and neither will you if you are not connected to Me."*

The original Greek word for abide is menō and means not to depart; to continue to be present; to be held, kept, continually. Are you remaining connected to Him 24–7?

Not always. I get distracted or do things that is not saying yes to him, but I am saying yes more often than before.

DAYTIME DARE

Do you trust Him? Are you convinced the current environment He placed you is where you can flourish and grow?
If so, dare to put more roots down. Take a step today to intentionally ask Him: "What are you after growing in me right now?" Write down what He says to you:

trust, love, passion, complete
Satisfaction, selflessness,
attention, obidience

E EVENING REFLECTION

"Trust in the Lord with all your heart and lean not on your own understanding; in all your ways submit to him, and he will make your paths straight." Proverbs 3:5–6

Our ability to grow good fruit is directly linked to how much we trust God. Do we believe He is a good gardener? Do we believe He has good intention and purpose for our lives? Take a moment to tell God you are choosing not to lean on your own understanding but to trust Him. Write down anything He says to you:

No one can love me like
he does hes the only person
who has treated me fully with
love, he is all I need, he
will fill me and reward me -
but I have to push through
the initial hardship, hes the
only stable thing I will always
have

DAY 7 : *The Seed*

"For a seed to achieve its greatest expression,
it must come completely undone. The shell cracks,
its insides come out and everything changes."
— Cynthia Occelli

It's amazing to look at nature and see what grows from a seed. Look at an oak tree; it comes from a tiny acorn! A seed is tiny, but once it is planted in good soil it has the potential to become something much larger.

In my relationship with God, I'm on a continual journey of learning to know the difference between what He holds me responsible for and what He's taking care of. As I pay attention to this, I find my life is manageable and do-able, knowing He's not expecting me to do what only He can do. Over the years I have learned that when I'm feeling overwhelmed it's usually because I have got the boundaries confused and I am trying to do God's part for Him! Do you do the same thing? Our spiritual life is a relationship. They say it 'takes two' to make a relationship work and 'they' are right! Each person in the relationship has a responsibility to that relationship to make it successful, but we are not called to do everything. To live that way would be unwise, unhealthy and would make us unhappy. In our relationship with God, He holds our lives in His hands and cares for us deeply, but we have responsibilities within our lives. Building a vibrant life requires understanding what's yours and stewarding and caring for it with all your heart.

So firstly, creating the 'seed' is God's responsibility and and it's ALWAYS good seed! There's not any bad seed in His hand.

Everything that any seed carries has the full potential to grow lasting fruit in your life; period! In Isaiah 55:11 God says, *"So it is when I declare something. My word will go out and not return to Me empty, but it will do what I wanted; it will accomplish what I determined."* (VOICE) So the Word of God, the Bible, His words, the things He speaks all have purpose, intention and power behind them. That means every single thing from the Word of God and in the Word of God is teeming with life, just looking for soil to land in. It's *impossible* for the Word of God to come up empty!

What's the best way to get seed in us? The 'how' we get the Word in us is not as important as the 'if'. If we want loads of fruit growing in every area of our lives, we need a *lot* of seed. We want abundance! We want to get the Word (seed) into our soil so we need to look for ways to sow it and have it planted.

The Bible tells us that seeds of faith get planted in us when we hear His Word (see Romans 10:17). I love this! It doesn't matter if it's through reading, listening, memorizing or meditating, it's all 'hearing'. Our ability to absorb the seed causes it to have its "greatest expression" (as the quote says above). He provides the seed of His Word and as we hear it, faith grows and the truth gets planted in us. It was meant to get in you. The Bible tells us that it's "living and active" (Hebrews 4:12) so it's going to grow and bear fruit!

 MORNING MEDITATION

Remember, our ability to make the seed is impossible but our ability to cultivate and help it grow is vital to our development. Choose your own scripture today to meditate on. Maybe it's one that has been 'on your heart' for a while. Ask God for a deeper revelation of its meaning for you personally in this season of your life.

stop comparing myself, remember we are all children of god

DAYTIME DARE

Take the scripture that you meditated on this morning into your day. The Lord is training you and wants to delight in showing you how this scripture is relevant to you right now. Take it with you and 'apply' it to all the situations that come your way.

EVENING REFLECTION

Consider your day. This morning you took the seed He offered you. As you went about your day you cultivated your soil and allowed that seed to get planted by applying it. As you look back now, what tiny (or large!) 'beginning' growth do you see?

my god will come through always realizing where I am not doing my part of this relationship, trying to be fully satisfied in him, finding moments to just focus on my love for him.

phil 2:2-5 agree wholeheartedly w/ one another, loving one another, working together. Don't be selfish; don't try to impress, think of others as better than self. Take interest in others not own.

"Affirmations are like seeds planted in soil. Poor soil, poor growth. Rich soil, abundant growth. The more you choose to think thoughts that make you feel good, the quicker the affirmations work."
— Louise L. Hay

"But the seed in the good soil, these are the ones who have heard the word in an honest and good heart, and hold it fast, and bear fruit with perseverance" Luke 8:15 (NASB). In this passage, Jesus explains what happens when the seed (the Word of God) lands on different types of soil. The "honest and good heart" is described as good soil.

The honest and good heart is a heart that hears the Word of God, trusts the author and takes it in immediately. At the moment that heart receives the seed, it purposes to hold on to it, believing that with perseverance it will grow good fruit.

The Word of God that is planted in a hearing heart also grows faith. Faith is fruit that comes from hearing the word of God ("the spirit of Truth" as Jesus calls it in John 16) with an honest and good heart.

In another scripture, a more complete picture is given: *"But examine everything carefully; hold fast to that which is good..."* (1 Thessalonians 5:21). The good soil when it hears the Word of God, will examine it carefully and hold fast to the good news it contains. It produces the fruit of faith, an *"...assurance of things hoped for, and a conviction of things not seen"* (Hebrews 11:1).

Is there more that can be produced in the good soil with the Word of God? Faith is only one of many fruits that are produced: "*But the fruit of the Spirit is love, joy, peace, patience, kindness, goodness, faithfulness, gentleness, self-control; against such things there is no law*" (Galatians 5:22, 23). This fruit is the development of God's character in us.

Yesterday we explored the fact that God is responsible for the seed. He is the one who makes it and He is the one who plants. *So, what's our responsibility when it comes to growth?* The soil! Yep … it's that simple! Without rich, soft, beautiful and nutritious soil the seed will die. It doesn't matter how amazing the seed is; it's impossible for it to grow without the proper environment.

(M) **MORNING MEDITATION**

Think about your personal responsibility to "care" for the Word of God in your life. Like the Psalmist said, "I have hidden your word in my heart that I might not sin against you." Psalm 119:11. The word "hide" in the original means *to store up treasure*. When you hide treasure, it's intentionally hidden so no one can take it. Are you able to hide God's Word in your heart today?

I have to constantly remind myself of his word. It is not yet automatic, but I hope with time it will constantly be hidden in me

DAYTIME DARE

One of the easiest ways to hide God's word in the heart is through Scripture memorization. Today I want you to memorize Psalm 119:11. Take a moment to write it down somewhere (Journal, bathroom mirror, 3 x 5 card, etc.) and say it aloud until you have committed it to memory.

I have hidden your word in my heart so that I. will not sin against you,

EVENING REFLECTION

Consider your day. Did you have a chance to store God's Word in your heart? Did what you read, memorize, or hear stay in your heart? Was it easily taken away by today's distractions and tomorrow's worries? Take a moment to quietly quote Psalms 119:11 under your breath, asking God to hide it in your heart.

He has given me the greatest gifts and knows me better than I do so why should I hide my heart from him. It is already his and it only hurts me to keep it from him.

"God is like the sun, in that He gives light and life to those on whom He shines; but the warmth of His love is hidden from those who remain under the dark cloud of sin."
—Ray Comfort

In order for a seed to germinate it requires sunlight. Even a flawless seed planted in well nourished soil cannot grow without light. The sun is the triggering mechanism for the seed, sending a wavelength of light reaching within the soil straight to the seed. It triggers the growth and development.

A seed that germinates in "darkness" requires a long wave-length light to do so. The light causes growth. It doesn't matter how deep the seed lays underground, if the sunlight can reach it ... it will grow! What spiritual truth can we learn from this? God's very presence and life-giving light can bring any seed to life no matter how dark the environment may be.

The Bible says that the Word of God never returns void. This means that when you have good seed planted in good soil (the Word in your heart) God will come and bring LIFE to it in time. In the right season it will come to life because it's impossible for it not to bear fruit.

Psalm 84:11 says, *"The Lord God is our sun and our strength: the Lord will give grace and glory: he will not keep back any good thing from those whose ways are upright."*

Part of that word *sun*, is a Hebrew word, *shemesh*, meaning PUBLIC. I love the thought of this! It's almost as if the writer is saying, "It's impossible for the SUN not to make public the Word inside of you."

Our ability to let the sun reach the seed that's within us is vital. Many times we are quick to rush out of God's presence without allowing the sunlight to reach the seed within us. One of the greatest ways we can allow God to develop His Word in us is to give time to it. It reminds me of a Dark Room; the room where a camera film is developed. This room requires darkness and allotted time for development to take place. I would like to suggest that the same happens in our hearts. There is no formula to having rapid growth but we can be sure of this: our ability to continually abide in the midst of His presence is linked to the depth of our growth. We can apply our faith to this principle. If we allow the seed to be planted in our hearts we must allow God time for His presence to develop it. When we overexpose it or rush the process, our soil is shallow and our growth will be shallow also. Never underestimate the time it takes for development and growth or you will be tempted to rush the process.

(M) MORNING MEDITATION

The Bible says that when Mary, the Mother of Jesus, heard the Word of God she hid it in her heart for the right time.

"But Mary was keeping within herself all these things (sayings), weighing and pondering them in her heart." Luke 2:19 (AMP)

There are things God speaks to us that require hidden time. Not everything He says needs to be out in the open because it requires time for development. If we rush to share what God has given us, we can create 'Joseph moments' in our lives. Wisdom is always speaking, so if you don't know what to share... ASK! God is always willing to help you in your time of need.

My heart needs time to bury
and hide gods word in my heart.
I can't expect revelation right
away, I need to plant myself
in God before he will transform
me and help me grow.

 **DAYTIME DARE**

Take a moment today to allow development in your heart. Find a place to go for a few minutes to hide away and pray. It may be your room, a closet, a bathroom or the car. It just needs to be someplace private where you can pray. Take a few minutes to tell God that you want His words to develop in your heart.

As a sign of worship lift your hands and say aloud, "God I am yours. I'm not going to rush out of Your presence or try and fast-forward the process. Take Your time! I'm all in. Do what you do best! Give me vibrant growth. Amen."

_____

_____

_____

_____

_____

_____

This morning we talked about hiding God's Word in our hearts. We took a moment in our day to ask Him to develop us. When you prayed this prayer what did you feel? Did you feel a sense of peace or anxiety? The purpose in prayer is to always give back what God has already given us. It's God's responsibility to develop the seed. Is there an area where you have taken on this responsibility? Take a moment to surrender it back to God and write down what He says:

So much peace. The seed
is already in me. I try
to ignore it and do things
my own way. God gave
me the seed right when I
asked/wanted but I disregarded

*"The world is all the richer for having a devil in it,
so long as we keep our feet upon his neck"*
— *William James*

It's impossible to talk about development without understanding that there are seasons in which we are sifted. What this means is that even if the seed is perfect, the soil is developed and the time for the sun to reach the seed is given, we still experience seasons that are unlike any other. We can experience a shaking that is not related to personal decisions or human activity. We don't always understand why something is happening to us when we are doing everything right. But we can look to the Word to understand a few truths.

First, we know that what the devil can't steal from us he will try and get us to give up to him. Many times it is the hard moments in life that shake us to the point where we surrender to him. It's often the confusion that sets in to our hearts. I love the phrase, *"God will oftentimes offend our mind to reveal our heart."*

Jesus explains in the book of Luke that this exact thing will be happening to Peter. It says, *"Simon, Simon, Satan has asked to sift all of you as wheat. But I have prayed for you, Simon, that your faith may not fail. And when you have turned back, strengthen your brothers."* Luke 22:31–32

The word *"sift"* in the Greek means, *"an inward agitation to try one's faith to the verge of overthrow."* The picture is someone who is being so shaken that they let go of what they are holding onto. Times of sifting can shake us to the core.

God allows sifting and it can strengthen us. One of the main characters in the Bible that we see this happen to is a man named Job. He had everything going for him! He was wealthy, powerful, happily married and a doting father. One moment everything was wonderful and the next moment he had lost everything. The Bible says Satan asked God if he could sift Job and God said yes. Even Job's friends told him to curse God and die. It must have been pretty bad for them to say something like this.

We can be confident that God is not punishing us but trusting us with the weight of such an experience. The Bible says that when we have to persevere we build our faith. *How many of us know that without having weight we don't build muscle?* I like to call it, 'building a history with God.' Your ability to build your own personal history with God gives you authority and authenticity. No one can take away your experience. If you have gone through hard things and God got you through it, that truth is forever etched into your heart and life. Everything that comes after that moment builds on this truth.

Just like in marriage, when you have your first argument you think that the relationship is falling apart and it feels like you might not come back from this moment. But once you are reconciled and life continues to move forward, you have more confidence in the robustness of the relationship. So the next time you're in an argument you have history that says, "You're going to be okay. This is not going to destroy your marriage."

God is the same way! We come to a crisis in our faith and He walks us through it. He continues to hold us, speak to us, and confirm His love for us. He walks us out of the "darkest valley" (Psalm 23). When we make it through a dark time we can turn and see that He never left us. The confidence we gain from knowing we can go through the darkest of times and trust His ability to hold us, gives us a perseverance and matures and deepens our faith.

(M) MORNING MEDITATION

King David wrote in Psalm 23, *"Even though I walk through the darkest valley, I will fear no evil, for you are with me; your rod and your staff, they comfort me."* Basically he is saying that no matter how destructive or devastating his circumstances are, he will not be taken out. One of the best ways to prepare for sifting in our life is to say no to fear. I love the phrase, *"We say no to fear and yes to love."* Our ability to say no to fearing what might come our way in life allows us to say yes to perfect love, which the Bible tells us, "drives out fear" (1 John 4:18). His love covers, empowers you and says, "I'm with you till the end." Take a moment and with your own mouth say aloud, "I say yes to love and no to fear!" How does that make you feel?

It feels good to trust him. It is a weight lifted off knowing that he will take care of me and get me through anything and that I will be rewarded with stronger faith from it.

(D) DAYTIME DARE

Today, when you come upon a situation where you experience fear, take a moment and under your breath say the phrase, "I'm going to say no to fear and yes to love." Make a conscious effort to expose fear in that moment and reach out for His love.

E EVENING REFLECTION

Did you get a chance to say yes to love today? Did you expose fear for what it is... a faith drainer? Take a moment and celebrate your progress! This week you learned about the Sower, the seed, the soil, the Sun, and the Sifter. Ask God to allow these foundational truths to become a part of your theology. Thank Him for your new knowledge!

Yes I have given him
my life which means
having no fear!

WEEK 3
Environments

Necessary Conditions

"A beginner must look on himself as one setting out to make a garden for his Lord's pleasure, on most unfruitful soil which abounds in weeds. His Majesty roots up the weeds and will put in good plants instead."
—*Saint Teresa of Avila*

We are all familiar with the Parable of the Sower and I touched briefly on the 'soil' of our hearts last week. I wanted to give some concentrated time to it this week and here's why: Soil needs attention to keep it good!

We can tend to look at the Parable and think that it only applies to the soil of our heart before we heard the gospel, and that once we came to accept Jesus we can say, "Oh, I'm the one with the fertile soil." No! I want to let you know that each of us have *all* the soils in our heart and we have got to get our hands dirty to keep it soft and fertile!

Anyone who loves to garden knows that soil needs regular tilling! I know when I started gardening I would dig the soil over, put fertilizer in it and admire how deep, rich and fertile it looked. Guess what? Months later when the season changed, I noticed a crusty hard surface and the soil was in clumps rather than soft and moist. Also, some weeds had grown up and they were affecting the flowers I was trying to grow. Keeping a garden looking good requires regular digging of the soil!

As our lives move forward, things happen to us and around us that can affect us and affect the condition of the soil in our hearts. Disappointment, hurt, anger, injustice, loss: all of these will leave us with hard, rocky, thorny, brittle or shallow soil that can't retain the seed God is giving us, unless we regularly come to the Lord, allowing Him to soften and massage those hard dry places with His oil of joy and water it with His living water.

Certain conditions and particular environments are necessary for growth. When a baby is born, it requires particular care for that stage of its development. If you don't care for the infant properly, it will not thrive. It's important to understand that not all environments and conditions lend themselves to growth. There are, and will be, environments and seasons that are perfect for your growth. Sometimes you will have to intentionally find them.

Remember you are responsible for your soil! You are responsible to care and nurture the seed God plants in you. Your soil is your heart and your life flows out from it.

Let's look a bit closer at Jesus' explanation of the meaning of the Parable of the Sower in Luke 8: 11–15. (NLT)

"The seed is God's word. The seeds that fell on the footpath represent those who hear the message, only to have the devil come and take it away from their hearts and prevent them from believing and being saved. The seeds on the rocky soil represent those who hear the message and receive it with joy. But since they don't have deep roots, they believe for a while, then they fall away when they face temptation (or the moment there's trouble). The seeds that fell among the thorns represent those who hear the message, but all too quickly the message is crowded out by the cares and riches and pleasures of this life. And so they never grow into maturity. And the seeds that fell on the good soil represent honest, good-hearted people who hear God's word, cling to it, and patiently produce a huge harvest."

It's so key for us to know the state of our soil. Where is it at? Is it hard, bare, shallow, full of thorns and rocks or is soft and rich and when you read the Word it goes straight in and takes root and produces fruit?

"How do I know?" you ask. Well, over the next few days we are going to look at each soil in turn so that with God's help we can 'till the soil' so that it's 'good' and is able to receive and grow the seed and produce fruit!

The soil in your life represents your heart. The Bible says, *"Above all else, guard your heart, for everything you do flows from it."* This is why understanding the state of your heart (soil) is so important. It gives you an understanding of how you treat the word when it comes your way. It's also the out-flow of your whole life. Your heart is the single most impor-tant thing to you, so don't rush this week. Take time to really ask God where your heart is. *Let Him speak to you!.*

 ## MORNING MEDITATION

Sit for a minute or two and quiet your spirit before the Lord. Put your hand on your heart and tell the Holy Spirit that you give Him full permission to show you today and this week which of the soil(s) you have in your heart. Tell Him that you want to 'till' the soil with Him because you want it all to be rich. Thank Him that He is going to do what you ask!

It will take constant
nourishing - I always have to
ask god to help me
nourish my soil.

DAYTIME DARE

I am sure, by now, that you are used to having the Holy Spirit prompt you and speak to you during the day. Today, specifically ask Him to prompt you at moments during the day and reveal to you the 'soil' in your heart. Write down what He says to you.

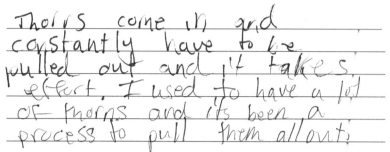

Thorns come in and constantly have to be pulled out and it takes effort. I used to have a lot of thorns and it's been a process to pull them all out.

EVENING REFLECTION

After giving him permission to show you the soil(s) in your heart, did you sense the Holy Spirit tilling the soil of your heart?* Did He show you something that surprised you? If so explain:

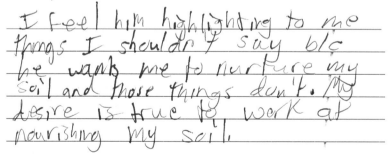

I feel him highlighting to me things I shouldn't say b/c he wants me to nurture my soil and those things don't. My desire is true to work at nourishing my soil.

* If you did not hear from God about your soil... Don't worry! We will spend the next four days explaining the soils and what your soil may look like. Just ask the Holy Spirit to highlight the specific soil you have each day. He will speak to you!

*"As he was scattering the seed, some fell along
the path, and the birds came and ate it up."
Matthew 13:4*

We are in an age where life feels more fast-paced. The birth of the Internet has given us Facebook, Twitter, and Instagram, all of which can leave us feeling like we are living an 'Instalife'! My husband, Ben, said the other day that he remembers the days of home telephones being attached to the wall and having cords (showing his age, I thought!) and there were no answering machines. If you called someone and they weren't at home you just had to call back. He went on to say that these days if you don't reply to someone's text within half an hour, they text saying, "Hello! Are you still alive?!"

Our hearts are meant to be rich fields the Lord can plant in, but with the busyness and 'instant response' age we live in, sometimes they are more like a well driven path. The soil becomes packed down and hard because all the information coming at us.

We read the Bible in the morning (or whenever we do) and a verse might stay a short while in our thoughts. We understand it. We believe it, but before long we have forgotten what we heard. The soil of our heart is so hard, by continual traffic, there is no hope for the seed to go deep and grow.

And when the seed stays on the surface of our hearts its easier for Satan to take it from us. He is constantly passing over your heart with his lusts, lies, and pride, hoping to devour the Word quickly!

Here are some signs of a Roadside Heart:

1. Are you inundated with spiritual things and yet nothing seems to stick?

2. Do you forget what the Bible says as soon as you walk away from it?

3. Do you have a hard time holding on to spiritual things (joy, hope, peace, etc.)?

(M) MORNING MEDITATION

Today we learned about the roadside soil. It's the soil that's so packed down by continual traffic that it's hard and dry. No matter how great the seed is, the soil has no ability to absorb the seeds any further than the surface. Does this sound like your life? Are you inundated with spiritual things and yet nothing seems to stick? Do you forget what the Bible says as soon as you walk away from it? Write down your thoughts:

> *Yes. somewhat. I am getting better at it. I am keeping his word in my heart more continually, but I still get drawn away by all the business in my life*

(D) DAYTIME DARE

Today try fasting from being inundated with information. Turn your phone off for parts of the day, don't open up your computer, or switch the TV on; choose to abstain from anything that hinders your ability to hear and receive more deeply from God. Take time to ask Him to cultivate your soil (heart). Ask Him to prepare your life to receive the Word that it might take root.

_____

_____

_____

_____

_____

_____

E **EVENING REFLECTION**

Reflect on the words Paul uses to challenge the church in Ephesians 4:32 (AMP)

"And become useful and helpful and kind to one another, tenderhearted (compassionate, understanding, loving-hearted), forgiving one another [readily and freely], as God in Christ forgave you."

I love how Paul uses the word tenderhearted! Part of being a true follower of Christ is aligning our hearts to be tender and respond quickly. A tender heart looks like someone who is compassionate and understanding.

Tonight, take a moment and ask the Lord to tenderize your heart. Ask Him to increase your ability to extend more compassion and give time to understand.

I give compassion often, but not always. I find it had to give compassion when someone does something over and over again.

DAY 13 : *Rocky Soil*

"Some fell on rocky places, where it did not have much soil. It sprang up quickly, because the soil was shallow."
Matthew 13:5 (NIV)

Today we'll explore what rocky soil looks like. It's important to note that again here, the Word was received with gladness. No one was trying to get rid of the seed, but there was a big problem! The soil was so full of rocks the seed couldn't find a place to grow. The state of the ground hindered the ability of the seed to go down deep and take root. *Was the seed good?* Yes. *Was the soil good?* Yes, but only partially good. The soil that was available was good but there was too little of it. It lacked depth and it was full of rocks.

This type of heart has a hard time letting things go. It's crowded with all kinds of things; worry, fear, offense, pain, unbelief, etc. It receives the Word gladly but has no ability to apply what it says because other things crowd it out.

Even if the seed begins to take root, the roots cannot go down deep. The seedling is in danger of getting taken out at the first sign of pressure. No matter how healthy the seedling may look, it will not last without roots. The danger of being rootless is far more dangerous than you may think. Plants that are rootless can look healthy on the outside. They can look lush, ready to bear fruit like any other plant. When the wind and the rain come they are knocked down. As quickly as they were built, they crumble to the ground. Just like a house built on sand.

Let's take a closer look at some of the rocks in our hearts that may be crowding out the Word ...

Offense takes up precious space in our hearts. Think of all the time, energy and peace it requires to hold on to offense? I love the quote; *"Life becomes easier when you learn to accept the apology you never got."* If you have hidden offense, it's time to let go ... It's time to forgive. It's time to pull some rocks out of your soil so God can grow the stuff you've been dreaming of.

Unbelief is another one of the 'rocks' that take up room. An unbelieving heart is an untrusting heart. Faith requires trust! When we have unbelief in our hearts, it chokes the faith right out of us.

Here are a few signs that you may have rocky soil in your heart:

1. Despite hearing and knowing the Word of God you still struggle with forgiving others on a regular basis.

2. Even though you hear a lot of the Word, your heart has grown weary from disappointment, pain, and offense so you don't allow it to take root.

3. You have been following Christ for some time but you haven't been able to go very deep in your experience with Him. You don't consider yourself to be as deep as a lot of Christians.

(M) **MORNING MEDITATION**

"I have swept away your offenses like a cloud, your sins like the morning mist. Return to me, for I have redeemed you."
Isaiah 44:22

Getting rid of offense is like de-cluttering your heart to make room. It's easier to forgive when we realize what we've been forgiven. Jesus took all of our offensive sin and washed them away... sweeping them away out of sight and into the sea of forgetfulness. Take a moment and just thank Him for the power of His forgiveness. Ask Him to make room in your heart by releasing forgiveness in your heart.

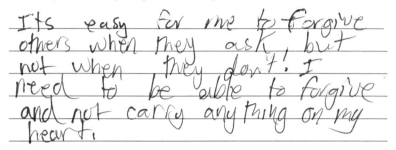

> It's easy for me to forgive others when they ask, but not when they don't! I need to be able to forgive and not carry anything on my heart.

 **DAYTIME DARE**

Today, recognize when offense tries to lodge in your heart. Take a moment and say to your heart, *"I see that's how I feel, but I don't have room for this offense in my heart. I only have room for the Word so, that's what I'm picking!"* Notice how much you have to choose this truth throughout the day.

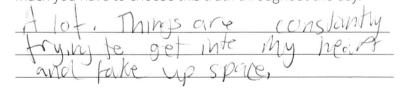

> A lot. Things are constantly trying to get into my heart and take up space.

E **EVENING REFLECTION**

Take a moment tonight and read these words in the book of Matthew. Think about what you're now building your life on. Thank God that His *Word is a safe place to land and a refuge.*

"These words I speak to you are not incidental additions to your life; homeowner improvements to your standard of living. They are foundational words, words to build a life on. If you work these words into your life, you are like a smart carpenter who built his house on solid rock. Rain poured down, the river flooded, a tornado hit—but nothing moved that house. It was fixed to the rock."

If my heart is filled w/ his word, I will be able to stand strong. Nothing else will be able to get into my life.

> *"Other seeds fell among thorns, and the thorns grew up and choked them out."*
> Matthew 13:7 (ESV)

Today we look at the Thorny soil! This soil, after it's been plowed and ready to receive seed, wasn't weeded enough. It wasn't prepared thoroughly. The roots of the weeds were not cleared completely and they were hidden under the soil.

This soil is like a person who God asked to get rid of things in their life. They began the process and outwardly resembled holiness but, deep down inside, their root system was not cleared out. The weeds could still grow!

When God speaks we need to listen! A few years back God began to speak to me about obedience. He began to challenge me to commit myself to 100% obedience. In our home we like to say, *"I need you to obey right away, all the way, and with a happy heart."* Obedience done without timeliness or half-heartedness is not full obedience. And if you do exactly what's asked of you, when it's asked, but lack a happy heart, then it's not full obedience.

This is what Jesus is talking about! He's talking about someone's heart where His work has begun but the roots of old patterns, sinful ways and deep-rooted addictions have not been broken. It looks clean on the outside, even having a picture of holiness, but it lacks purity. The full work of renewal has not taken place.

Sometimes we believe things are not dangerous to our growth, but if God asks you to get rid of it, it's important that we obey. He is the only one that knows what can jeopardize our growth in Him. He is the only one who can see into the future. If God is asking you to rid yourself of things, obey! *Don't delay*! *Obey with a happy heart*! His intentions toward you are perfect and He would never ask you to get rid of something unless He has a full purpose in it.

Here are a few signs you may have Thorny soil in your heart:

1. You have heard the word with gladness and began the process of renewal but haven't allowed yourself to go all the way.

2. You're a great starter but you lack follow-through in your spiritual life.

3. God has asked you to get rid of certain things in your life (relationships, addictions, sin) and you've been slow to respond or you have no intention of responding.

(M) **MORNING MEDITATION**

"And this is love: that we walk in obedience to his commands. As you have heard from the beginning, his command is that you walk in love." — 2 John 1:6

This morning, think about how your obedience demonstrates your love for the Lord. Offer Him your full heart and all that's within it. Commit to following Him in full obedience today.

Is there something God's putting his finger on today? Explain:

Loving others, not letting disappointment/
anger/annoyance into my heart,
Fully trusting him and therefore
not worrying

DAYTIME DARE

We are on the theme of obedience. Today, purpose in your heart to obey God all the way. When God asks you to do something, do it with your whole heart! Tell your soul to obey God. Don't try to reason or explain your way out of full obedience. Just tell your soul, *"If God said it, then I'm doing it!"*

_____

_____

_____

_____

_____

_____

EVENING REFLECTION

"If you tell God no because He won't explain the reason He wants you to do something, you are actually hindering His blessing. But when you say yes to Him, all of heaven opens to pour out His goodness and reward your obedience. What matters more than material blessings are the things He is teaching us in our spirit."
— Charles Stanley

Tonight, think about those things God is asking you to obey Him in. How did you do today? What were some things that made it difficult to obey Him? Write down the feelings you had once you purposed to obey.

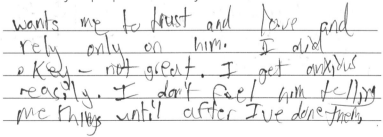

wants me to trust and love and
rely only on him. I did
okay - not great. I get anxious
reasily. I don't feel him telling
me things until after I've done them.

DAY 15 : *Roadside Soil*

"Still other seed fell on good soil, where it produced a crop—a hundred, sixty or thirty times what was sown."
Matthew 13:8

Today we look at the good soil! This soil is perfect for growth. It's primed and ready to build a harvest. It flourishes in the Fall and stores up for the Winter. I think it's safe to say we ALL want this type of soil.

"The ground is described as "good"— not that it was good by nature, but it had been made good by grace. God had plowed it; he had stirred it up with the plow of conviction, and there it lay rich and soft as it should be. When the seed was planted, the heart received it, for the heart said, "That is just the blessing I want." So that the hearing of the word was THE thing to give comfort to this plowed soil. Down fell the seed to take good root."

What can good seed produce? It produces fervency of love, largeness of heart, a humble spirit, a desire to learn, passionate purpose, etc. It's limitless in nature. Whatever you need has the ability to grow in this soil, giving you a well-nourished life full of possibility and potential.

It also produces seed that reproduces the same fruit! It continues to grow in aptitude. You may have planted a small seed of hope, faith, peace, etc. The seed will give you a harvest but not only that ... it will give you more seeds to plant and produce a larger harvest. Sometimes giving you a hundredfold of what you planted. This is what maturity in God looks like. Seasons and seasons of producing fruit ... Growing in harvest. Growing in capacity. Growing in grace.

BY HAVILAH CUNNINGTON · 67

Jesus promises an increase when we have good soil, because He can keep on sowing into us and we will reap and reap and be fruitful.

(M) MORNING MEDITATION

"Therefore, you will fully know them by their fruits."

Jesus explains that you will know a true follower by the fruit in their life. Their fruit tells a story of what seeds they have planted. Fruit does not lie!

Today, take a moment and think about your own fruit. What fruit are you seeing that you really are happy about? What seeds did you plant to get this fruit? *Write it down:*

love to put others above
myself and be selfless
trust and hope from knowing
god will take care of me

What fruit are you discouraged about?
What seeds did you plant to get this fruit? *Write it down:*

physical impulses from unmet
love needs
emotional impulses from lack
of true stability in god

DAYTIME DARE

Today, buy a pack of seeds. It doesn't matter what kind you get — just buy a simple pack. Place this pack of seeds in a visual place. (Bathroom mirror, car dashboard, on your refrigerator, etc.) Each time you see this pack of seeds, say a simple prayer, *"Lord, help me to plant the right seeds!"*

EVENING REFLECTION

"The [uncompromisingly] righteous shall flourish like the palm tree [be long-lived, stately, upright, useful, and fruitful]; they shall grow like a cedar in Lebanon [majestic, stable, durable, and incorruptible]." Psalm 92:12 (AMP)

No matter what your seed looks like ... No matter your harvest, you have a chance to start fresh today! Tonight, take a moment and just thank God that His purpose in your life will not end. He is fully engaged in this process. He's not watching from afar. He's not disappointed at your soil. He's HOPEFUL. He knows what can be done when soil is prepared for good seed. Take a moment to just worship Him! Write down anything He speaks to you:

You will get there just put
everything in the seed of
Friendship, don't let
anything other than him dictate me,

WEEK 4
Development

Stages & Seasons
"Every moment and every event of every man's
life on earth plants something in his soul."
— Thomas Merton

Growth can be traced through "Stages of Development." Each stage is vital and cannot be skipped. They are predictable and normative phases to spiritual growth. Don't worry, all mature Christians have passed through these stages. It's important to have grace for yourself and for others who may be working their way through them. It's not always pretty!

Seasons in God are inevitable! Just as they occur in our natural world, so it is for us spiritually; we experience winter, spring, summer, and fall. We also experience seasons in the other parts of our lives, too; including ministry, marriage, business, finances, relationships, etc.

Without an ability to discern the time or season that we are in, we are susceptible to being led astray, changing our minds, making rash decisions, hearing incorrectly, looking for a 'harvest' in our lives when in fact we are in winter (and blaming ourselves for lack of growth.) It can sometimes mean that we miss what God is doing in and with us in the specific season.

It is vitally important that you are able to discern the season you are in! It's your responsibility to hear God and to protect your harvest through every season. Don't worry, you are not doing this alone... He will help you!

"For everything that happens in life — there is a season, a right time for everything under heaven: A time to be born, a time to die; a time to plant, a time to collect the harvest; A time to kill, a time to heal; a time to tear down, a time to build up"
Ecclesiastes 3:1–3 (VOICE)

It's impossible to serve God for any period of time without facing different seasons, so you can see why it is vitally important to know which season you are in.

This week, we are going to look at each of the four natural seasons—winter, spring, summer, fall—and explore what they look like when applied to our spiritual life. My hope is that in doing this, it will help make sense of some of the feelings and attitudes we have and choices we make in each season.

Again, everything comes back to trust. If we believe that God is only around in the summer and that when winter arrives He leaves us, we will abandon ship! It's important to have a set of core values that we live by when it comes to understanding and navigating different seasons or we won't weather them well.

Here are some core values for you to think about today:

1. **God will be FAITHFUL to you.** Faithfulness is an intrinsic part of God's nature. He can't help Himself but to be faithful to you!

2. **God is FULLY aware of your season.** You are never alone no matter how dark a season you may be in. *He is there with you!*

3. **God is ALL POWERFUL** in every season. He is so powerful that He has the ability to meet every single need you have; even the needs you have going on in the tougher seasons. *He can reach you!* He is more than able to guide you through the season you're in.

4. **God is WORKING everything out!** He promises He is working everything you are going through for your good because you love Him and are called according to His purpose. Just because you can't see the end doesn't mean He can't. *Hold on and have faith!*

5. **Seasonal change will eventually COME!** Hold on. Your life is not going to stay in one season. He is making a way through for you and your season *will* change. Nothing lasts forever. You can be sure the sun will rise on a new season. *Trust God!*

 MORNING MEDITATION

"And I am convinced and sure of this very thing, that He Who began a good work in you will continue until the day of Jesus Christ [right up to the time of His return], developing [that good work] and perfecting and bringing it to full completion in you." Philippians 1:6 (AMP)

The Hebrew word for "*convinced*" is the word "*persuaded*" but it carries the idea of being so persuaded that you are moved to do something. You have to act!

My question today for you is ... Are you persuaded God is with you?

Does your persuasion exert you to trust Him? Explain.

I know that hes supposed
to be, but I don't live
as if I truly believe it.
I have to remind myself
he is and that I can trust
him.

 DAYTIME DARE

Take a moment and think about the season you're in. You might know exactly what season you are in or you might not be very clear. If you do know, find a picture that represents the season for you and post it somewhere so that you see it on a daily basis (screensaver, desktop wallpaper, Facebook cover photo, refrigerator, bathroom mirror, etc.) Let this picture speak to you, encourage you and confirm that God is with you in this season. Write down the season you believe you're in.

winter/spring, they coming
out of winter into spring. My
ground is warming to God,
but my soil needs work to
be able to nourish a seed

Take a moment to review the core values we read about this morning. Evaluate your heart to see if there's one you need more faith for. Ask God to give you a deeper revelation in your heart in order that you can own these core values as your own. Write down the one that stands out the most to you and why.

need to trust his faithfulness and that he will work everything out and that seasons change will come. hardest b/c things have been tough and so many things haven't worked out and a lot of change is going to come soon,

DAY 17 : *Winter: Waiting Well*

"In the depth of winter I finally learned that there was in me an invincible summer."
— *Albert Camus*

Winter is an interesting and unique season to be in. It almost feels like the opposite of everything we should be experiencing as a Christian. *Let's be honest...* In our minds, the vibrant life doesn't look like a vast, barren landscape with very little sign of life. Winter can be a difficult season because there is little (obvious) activity; and if you find yourself in it, you will know. King David was a man who wrote about seasons and in some of his favorite Psalms he described the winter season perfectly. Like in Psalm 63:1 (NIV):

"You, God, are my God, earnestly I seek you; I thirst for you, my whole being longs for you, in a dry and parched land where there is no water." *"Dry and parched land"* doesn't sound like summer! Those words in the Hebrew paint the picture of a man who has been on a journey only to find himself in a desert. David is weary, he is tired, and we see him crying out to God. He is saying that, more than his own personal hunger and thirst, his soul hungers and thirsts for God.

In winter, it's very difficult to see any growth in our lives because there is nothing obvious to see. Things can feel like they are dead, when, in fact, they are just dormant and there is change happening underneath the surface.

If you find yourself in winter... *don't worry*! Here are some things you can actively do in order to thrive in this important season.

Winter can be an uncomfortable time. Don't try to find comfort in things that will eventually hurt you. It's impossible to deeply comfort your soul and spirit through external, physical means. Purpose in this time to dig deep in your spirit and find comfort in the Comforter!

Winter is a time to be intimate with God. Because this season lends itself to feelings of isolation, be intentional to share the deeper longings of your heart with God. Even if it's hard in this time to feel His closeness as you have in previous seasons, He is just as close to you and still listening.

Winter is a time to rest physically. The other three seasons require more work to plant and harvest. Winter is quiet and dormant. Take advantage of this season! Store up rest ... Spring is coming!

Winter is a time to live on what has been stored from previous harvests. Winter is a season where we can draw living water from the wells we have dug with God and nourish ourselves from the storehouses we have filled. What we have built in God up until this point will be required during this season. Revisit those times with God; remind yourself of the richness you encountered. Do you have specific encounters? Spend time meditating on the promises God has set over your life. They will mean more to you during this season.

Winter is a time of gaining direction for plowing. Along with the seeming dryness of this season, the ability to sort through the kind of harvest you would like to reap in the next season is within your reach. Ask God to show you what soil needs plowing in your heart and what you need to plant. Look to Him for fresh seeds.

Winter is a time to glean from past mistakes. If you don't like your harvest, i.e., if the fruit you are displaying is distasteful — then you need to change what you are sowing into your life. It's as simple as that! If there are things that need to be corrected, then this is the time to plow the ground and plant differently.

(M) **MORNING MEDITATION**

"The sluggard does not plow when winter sets in; therefore he begs in harvest and has nothing." Proverbs 20:4 (AMP) Do you find yourself in a winter season? If so, what is God asking you to plow and plant today?

coming out of winter and into spring — wants me to start nourishing my soil and make it soft — wants me to start preparing for my sprout

DAYTIME DARE

Today is all about understanding the season of winter. Sometimes when we go through winter seasons in God, we can have a tendency to allow lies and unbelief to harden the soil in our hearts. Revisit the "signs of winter" above and ask God to reveal any lie you may have believed about His presence during your wintertime.

hes not there, he won't make things better for me he doesn't have better thing in store for me

E EVENING REFLECTION

"Look, the winter is past, and the rains are over and gone"
Song of Songs 2:11 (NLT)

Take a moment and thank God that winter will eventually give way to spring... *the sun will shine again!* Thank Him for sustaining you in this season.

Write down something He has done to sustain you in this season:

he has given me a girls group and family Jesse to show me what spring is

*"She turned to the sunlight and shook her yellow head,
and whispered to her neighbor: "Winter is dead."*
— A.A. Milne

Thank God for spring! Spring is a season for new growth and new beginnings. Each of us will experience these seasons in God because He is committed to our growth and fruitfulness! These are times when we experience heaven's fresh rain falling on our dry land. And this is a sovereign moment in time; a time when what we have planted will begin to grow and what we hope for will spring forth. It's one of those seasons where we have to take full advantage of the momentum of growth before it's too late.

If you find yourself in springtime, here are a few things you want to be aware of so you can make the most of the season.

Spring is a time of planting and activity. *It's time to get your hands dirty!* It's time to intentionally pull the Word into the soil of your life. You'll need to be strategic and intentional. *It's time to get busy!* If you continue to stay in hibernation, like your last season, you will miss an opportunity for substantial growth; growth that can happen in a very short period of time.

Spring is a time for work and effort to carry out instructions given in winter. Now that you've looked at your past regrets and evaluated the bad seed you may have sown, it's time to purposely plant! Don't expect this to be easy even if the sun is beginning to shine. It will take a methodical and patient plan to prepare for summer.

Spring is a time of plowing new ground. Some of the things you will need to do may feel a bit like plowing through hard ground. *But don't worry!* The ground is ready to be turned over because the time of hibernation was enriching your soil. Get in there and uproot unforgiveness, bitterness, idolatry, pride, etc. The ground is ready for these weeds to be pulled but it will take some work.

 MORNING MEDITATION

Part of plowing your ground in preparation of new seed is also preparing to protect the infant growth of the new seedlings. Today, think about ways you can protect the growth that is happening in your life. Here is an example: "Wise choices will watch over you. Understanding will keep you safe."
Proverbs 2:11 (NLT)

cut things out of my life that
inhibit the seed, sin, people
that do not foster my growth,
worry, bitterness, frustration,
focus only on the word of
god

DAYTIME DARE

If wise choices will protect, then it's important that we under-stand what that means. In another translation it says 'discre-tion', which means 'avoiding words or actions resulting in an unwanted consequence.' Is there something you are doing today where you can practice discretion?

the way I deal with others,
the way I handle stress,
when I am not saying yes
or loving others

Can you protect the new growth in your life in a better way?

Focus more on god and
his word, fill my heart
with him and nothing else,
Keep my emotions from
getting in the way

EVENING REFLECTION

Take a moment and thank God for this season of new growth and new beginnings. Thank Him for the infant stages of harvest and His faithfulness to you. *What makes this season so special to you? Is there something you would like to remind yourself about?*

This is the time to take God in and learn - getting to prepare for growth is exciting Knowing that you will grow

"And so with the sunshine and the great bursts of leaves growing on the trees, just as things grow in fast movies, I had that familiar conviction that life was beginning over again with the summer."
— *F. Scott Fitzgerald*

Summer is a season of fulfillment! The winter has passed and the sun is shining. All the things that have been done in secret are now clear for everyone to see. It's a moment in time where we are able to benefit from all the hard work we demonstrated. It is God's faithfulness bringing to light His sovereign provision in our lives. *There is evidence!* Summer is a time when we get to enjoy the reward of our labor.

But with every season there are potential dangers that we must be aware of and with abundance always comes the threat of distraction. Distractions can cause us to overlook or neglect the things that are necessary even in a season of fulfillment. Just like in a marriage; when you're enjoying a great season, it doesn't mean that you can be complacent and stop giving to the other person. It doesn't mean that you stop sowing into their life. You sow in and out of season!

Summer is a time for watering. Watering in the Bible is linked to prayer and we all know that prayer is simply having conversation with God. In the season of summer, it's vital that we water our relationship with God. Continuing to thank Him for a season in which you get to harvest! Daily spiritual discipline is just as vital now as it was in the winter.

Summer is a time for weeding the freshly planted crop.
All fresh crops have the threat of weeds. Weeds would love
to choke your new growth and suck all the nutrients from the
fresh new plants. *We need to be alert!* Not everything that is
green is healthy. It's important to survey the soil of your heart
each day; pulling things out that have the potential to harm
your harvest. Even an incredible looking garden that has
been well planted and watered is under threat from weeds.

 MORNING MEDITATION

*"He who gathers crops in summer is a prudent son, but he who
sleeps during harvest is a disgraceful son."* Proverbs 10:5 (NIV)

If you find yourself in the season of summer, it's time to take
advantage of the season you are in and gather your 'crops'.
As fun as it is to be in a season of refreshing and renewal,
we must be prudent to store truth in our hearts for seasons
ahead. Is there something you can do during this season to
help you store up truth?

Meditate on his word, focus
on god through everything,
continue to read, watch videos,
church and city groups.

 **DAYTIME DARE**

Sometimes our internal season is different than our external circumstances. We can be going through a spiritual dryness and yet have financial abundance. Sometimes we can be spiritually alive and physically be in a wintertime. Today, find a way to harvest something. Offer it to God as an offering of worship. It could be a prayer, a financial gift, or an act of service.

_____

_____

_____

_____

_____

_____

E **EVENING REFLECTION**

Summer is a season of blessing and abundance but we must remember to water what we have. Take some time to talk to God tonight. Ask Him to continue to fill and refresh you with the living water of His word and presence. Give Him permission to nurture what He has planted. Write down anything He said to you:

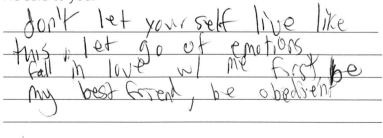

don't let yourself live like this, let go of emotions fall in love w/ me first, be my best friend, be obedient

*"Let us not become weary in doing good, for at the
proper time we will reap a harvest if we do not give up."*
Galatians 6:9

Fall is a season of promise! After a long season of work and effort, we now have abundance. If we didn't grow weary in well doing, we are set to reap a harvest. Fall is the time of harvest. It's a time when we gather the fruit of our labor and store it up for the winter to come.

FALL is a time where the physical evidence of our hard work during previous seasons materializes. I love the phrase, "Don't judge each day by the harvest you reap, but by the seeds that you plant." This is what Fall is about. It's the tangible proof of the seeds you have been sowing. Remember, there is no such thing as overnight success, just like there is no such thing as an overnight harvest. So, if you have a harvest... *CELEBRATE! You planted the right seeds!*

FALL is a time of thanksgiving. It's a wonderful season of Sabbath. Sabbath in the Hebrew denotes celebration. In Genesis when it says, "God rested on the seventh day," it means God sat back and celebrated His creation. We are created by God to do the very same thing. We need to have a season of celebration and celebrate the face that we made it! We also need to have a grateful heart, thanking God for the seed He gave us. He was faithful to complete the work He started ... *just like He promised!*

FALL is a time to store up because winter is coming.
We must not forget to stockpile the goodness of God; we will
need it in the days to come. Taking time to write down what
the Lord has done or sharing with someone will help store
it in our hearts. It's a season to gather all the abundance we
are experiencing and savor the season. We are responsible
to create an adequate store for the future.

**FALL is a time for stewardship and giving away what
has been harvested.** It's time to give away some of what you
have grown. You should have more than enough for yourself
and those around you and it's time to bless others. If God
has given you favor then use that favor to bless others. If
God has given you finances then use those funds to bless
others. If God has given you physical health then use your
energy to serve others. Don't be afraid to give some of your
harvest away, God will multiply your seed next time... *it's a
promise!*

 MORNING MEDITATION

*"Go to the ant, you sluggard; its ways and be wise! It has no
commander, no overseer or ruler, yet it stores its provisions in
summer and gathers its food at harvest."* Proverbs 6:8 (NIV)

Are you in the season of Fall? Has God given you an
amazing harvest?

Not in full but he still
gives me things I need, food
money a job school

Are there things that you can do to store up some of what God has given you? Take a moment to write them down:

write down the blessings - family, house, school, job, money, food, friends, intelligence, health and remember these things

 **DAYTIME DARE**

Take some of your abundance and give it away! Buy someone a coffee or send someone a nice text message. Wherever you are feeling an abundance in your life ... give some away! Find someone who is in a winter season and bless their socks off! The only way to harvest next year is to sow seeds again.

E **EVENING REFLECTION**

Today is all about understanding where your treasure is. You will have evidence that you stored it in the right place if your harvest is healthy. The Bible reminds us to store up treasure where moth and rust will not destroy. It's safe to store up things in heavenly places. It's safe to invest in eternal life. Take a moment and evaluate how you did today. Did it feel great to bless someone?

I think my blessing was through love and it felt great to just love and have fun with others

Where have you been storing your time, talents, and treasures? Ask God to help you store them safely!

school, work somewhat in god but not as fully as I should.

WEEK 5
Maturity

Maintaining Your Garden

"A garden requires patient labor and attention. Plants do not grow merely to satisfy ambitions or to fulfill good intentions. They thrive because someone expended effort on them."
— *Liberty Hyde Bailey*

Progressing through all stages of development can only be considered successful growth. There are NO short cuts when it comes to full maturity. We may make it to our promised land sooner than 40 years but we all have to walk through the desert. Maturity isn't a gift ... it's a process. Have faith. *You may not be where you want to be but... You're on your way!*

The Book of James gives us a finish line that's hard to miss. The author says it this way:

"Let perseverance finish its work so that you may be mature and complete, not lacking anything." James 1:4 (NIV)

What can we understand about spiritual maturity?

1. **Spiritual Maturity is Possible.** The Hebrew word for "*mature*" describes a complete work. This is how our life in Christ works! The cross of Christ gave us the ability to live an abundant life. Maturity is knowing what seed is being planted, where it is planted, how much to water it, and when to harvest. James is not only saying to strive for it but to live from it.

2. **Maturity is Living from Wholeness.** The word "maturity" also holds the meaning "to mend." The picture it paints is like a garment that was ripped, but is now mended. It shows us that no matter how ripped or broken our beginning was, we can be mended to the extent that we are free to live an abundant life.

3. **Maturity is a Place of Lacking Nothing.** You're called to be a skilled farmer! God created you to walk out into your garden and know how to tend it in such a way that you are constantly growing fruit. You have been given EVERY-THING you need to live a vibrant life.

4. **Maturity is a steadfastness.** An ability to stand in every season is a mindset; a partnership with the Holy Spirit and a sweet surrender to His leading.

This week we will look at growing the right things in our life! We will seek to prepare, water and protect. We will be responsible.

When we lack something... We will nurture the right seeds!

When we experience winter... We will hope for summer!

When our seeds are prematurely dying... We will tend to our soil to protect them.

DAY 21 : Sowing Hope

"Any area that you don't have hope is an area that is under the influence of a lie."
—*Bill Johnson*

In the dictionary we find a simple meaning for the word hope: "To FEEL that something desired MAY happen." The words "feel" and "may" are two very indefinite and vague words. The dictionary definition of the word "hope" is NOT the Biblical hope we are talking about.

"May your unfailing love be with us, Lord, even as we put our HOPE in you." Psalm 33:22 (NIV)

Hope in this verse is the Hebrew word, *"yachal"* meaning "trust."

"Israel, put your HOPE in the Lord, for with the Lord is unfailing love and with him is full redemption." Psalm 130:7 (NIV)

Again this is the same Hebrew word, "trust."

How do we build Biblical hope? We choose to trust. We use our free will to agree with what the Spirit is saying. The Holy Spirit is always declaring, "You can trust God. He's worthy of trust. He does not lie. Only truth is in Him. Put your TRUST in Him." Our ability to choose trust, builds hope. When we lack hope, we lack trust. Hopelessness is a clear sign that we have insufficient trust.

In Psalm 62:5 (NIV) David said, "Yes, my soul, find rest in God; my hope comes from Him." I love how the Amplified version says it, "...for my hope *and* expectation are from Him." Hope is an expectation that God is going to do what He promised to do.

I think it's safe to say HOPE is having an expectant trust. Not a boring, "half-hearted" type of belief, but a lively, eager, whole-hearted and excited trust.

(M) MORNING MEDITATION

Hope is a joyful anticipation that something good is coming!
—*Kris Vallotton*

Do you have "joyful anticipation" for the day ahead? Can you surrender your will to God, asking Him to help you trust Him?

> I know he will take care of
> me but its so hard to see that
> its hard to be joyful right now.

(D) DAYTIME DARE

Take a moment to think about an area in your life where you lack hope. It could be a job, relationship, health issue, financial stability, etc. Write down the area you are most worried about below. Once you are done writing, write the word TRUST over the top of it in large letters. Take time to see the word TRUST over that area!

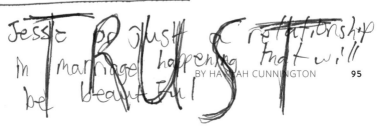

Jesse & I just a relationship
in marriage happening that will
be beautiful!

EVENING REFLECTION

This morning we explored how to grow HOPE in our lives. We saw the parallel between our trust and our hope. Take a moment to read the Message version of Psalm 62:5–6 and write down anything that God is highlighting.

"God, the one and only—I'll wait as long as he says. Everything I hope for comes from him, so why not? He's solid rock under my feet, breathing room for my soul, An impregnable castle: I'm set for life."

It comes just wait – he gives me everything so all I can do is wait for him patiently and glady cause no matter what I have to wait so make the wait god

Faith is a force to be reckoned with! It's the defining characteristic of a Christ follower. In Hebrews 11:6 (NIV) the Bible says that "...without faith it's impossible to please God." I would like to say it another way: 'It's impossible to see God without faith.' Faith is so powerful that when we declare what we believe in faith, mountains move and storms are stilled! The wind and waves of turmoil and trouble respond immediately, and disease and sickness have to leave. *That's some powerful stuff!*

In order for us to grow our faith, we have to understand a few things regarding faith. First, we know that if we lack "seeds" of faith we can ask for more and He will give us more! It's simply being willing to ask but not just ask; to ask with the grain of faith that we already have. If we believe He will increase our faith by asking for it we will already be putting our "mustard seed" of faith towards our mountain of unbelief.

Secondly, we know faith comes by hearing the Word of God. I love the Bill Johnson quote, *"We become what we behold."* According to the Bible we reflect what we see, so when we gaze at God, we begin to reflect Him. When we are looking at the world we will be tempted to take on an image that reflects our culture. Our pursuit of purposeful hearing will cause our faith to grow exponentially. Listening, reading, meditating or singing God's word will expand our faith and enable us to rise above our circumstances.

Growing faith from the inside and having it confirmed on the outside is like having the same radio station playing in different rooms of the house. It confirms what the Holy Spirit is saying to us internally and we see that God is consistent with what He is saying to us. This increases our faith and expectancy and therefore our capacity to hear the voice of God.

If you lack faith today, don't worry.... Ask for more!

If your faith is small, don't worry.... Use what you have and it will grow!

 MORNING MEDITATION

The first time FAITH is mentioned in the New Testament is when Jesus says to his listeners, *"If that is how God clothes the grass of the field, which is here today and tomorrow is thrown into the fire, will he not much more clothe you—you of little faith?"* Matthew 6:30 (NIV)

In the original Greek, the phrase, "...you of little faith" means, *"trusting too little."* Jesus makes a direct link between faith and trust. Think about the verse that says, *"For we live by faith, not by sight."* 2 Corinthians 5:7 (NIV)

Is there an area in your life where you are living by what you see in the physical or natural realm? Are you allowing your "spiritual" eyes to see God's perspective of that same area? If not, ask Him to open your eyes to see.

school and relationships - I get crowded vision of the earth and what I don't have right now instead of having complete trust in Gods future for me

DAYTIME DARE

I heard this phrase once and love it, "Fear is having faith in the wrong kingdom!" Today, take a moment today to purposefully put your faith in God and His kingdom perspective! Put on some worship music, go for a walk, close out distractions and position yourself to see God.

_____

_____

_____

_____

_____

_____

E EVENING REFLECTION

Today we explored how to grow faith. How did you do? Did you grow in your confidence? The Bible says, *"Now faith is confidence in what we hope for and assurance about what we do not see."* Hebrews 11:1 (NIV) Allow the seeds of what God can and will do, to go deep into your soil. Let Him speak to you. What is He saying?

He will carry me through the storm if I allow him, I need to put on the armour of god

"Gratefulness may be humanity's most underestimated devotional tool. We often forget that gratitude is how we access God's presence."
— Graham Cooke: The Language of Promise

Biblical gratitude is much different than just being thankful. Gratitude involves seeing things from a different angle, a new perspective. In the same way that a filter changes our view of something, gratitude helps us see things differently. Jesus said that He came so that we *"...may have and enjoy life, and have it in abundance (to the full, till it overflows)."* John 10:10 (AMP). Abundant life is not just something we are living for, but a position that we are meant to live *from*. Gratitude gives us a new context and framework to process life's circumstances from. The context is that we have been given the ability (through Jesus) to experience abundant living. With this filter, we can now view the world and our circumstances with a different 'lens'.

Gratitude allows us to feel a shift, without anything changing but our perspective. It gives us an ability to see the bigger picture and to see the hand of God at work in our life. We all know that sometimes we have to step back from something to see it more clearly. Gratitude allows us to pull back from life's circumstances and see it through His eyes.

So where do we grow gratitude? We grow gratitude in our minds and our hearts. Gratitude grows really well in our lives when we take time to meditate on the goodness of God; when we begin to agree with what the Spirit is saying rather than what our eyes are seeing. The mind of a Christian is a focused and disciplined mind; a pure and godly mind. This mind focuses on what it has rather than what it doesn't have. It refuses to dwell on what it is missing. It thanks God for His blessings and believes Him for increase.

Let me be clear: we are constantly in need of renewing our thinking. This doesn't mean just 'putting in' scripture, it also means proactively rejecting some thoughts. The enemy comes to "kill, steal and destroy," (John 10:10) and would love nothing more than to choke gratitude from our lives by throwing our natural circumstances at us. But we don't live by facts alone ... *we live by faith!*

Ask yourself this question: Do my thoughts magnify the goodness of God? Does He get bigger in my mind or smaller? God's ability is never in question because it never changes. He is good all the time and His power is limitless. There is no limitation to God and what He can do even if your mind, your circumstances and your enemy tries to tell you differently.

MORNING MEDITATION

Today it's time to put on your gratitude glasses! It's time to filter your life, circumstances, and relationships through the limitless possibilities of your heavenly Father.

In Psalm 34:3 David says, *"O magnify the Lord with me, and let us exalt His name together."* The Hebrew word for magnify is 'gadal' and means "to grow up." The author is saying we need to grow up into the goodness of God until the reality of His goodness becomes our joy and our strength. When you choose to agree with the Spirit that God is good and that He is in a good mood no matter what else is happening in your life, you are in a place of strength and He has become your refuge and your strong tower (Psalm 61:3) and *the enemy has a hard time penetrating your defenses!*

Are you 'growing up' into the goodness of God today?
Write down your thoughts.

I have to constantly remind
myself so it isn't first
nature yet but being thankful
for him and loving him
is my main goal

 **DAYTIME DARE**

Today is a great day to begin something called a 'Gratitude Journal.' This can be done in a book, on your phone, or in a voice memo. It doesn't have to be long, but just take a moment to write down one thing you are grateful for. Remember, you are trying to build the habit of gratitude. *This will help!*

E EVENING REFLECTION

"Praise the Lord. Give thanks to the Lord, for he is good; his love endures forever." Psalm 106:1 (NIV)

We focused on growing gratitude today. We learned that gratitude is a mindset and a way of 'seeing' that we choose based on what we know of God. The most grateful people in life are not those that have the most but those that choose to see from that perspective. The wonderful thing is that when we choose an 'attitude of gratitude,' we get to operate with the power of Holy Spirit. God's Spirit is always leading us into abundant living. When we choose to look at our daily life with the filter of gratitude, in light of eternity, things begin to shift. So tonight, take a moment and think about this. Write down anything you think God is saying to you.

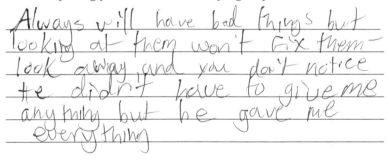

Always will have bad things but
looking at them won't fix them —
look away, and you don't notice
He didn't have to give me
anything but he gave me
everything

"Till some Truth into the soil of your heart
to make you reach for more."
—*Kim Walker-Smith*

In order for us to build strong lives in God we must first know the truth. In John 8:31–32 (NIV) Jesus says, *"If you hold to my teaching... Then you will know the truth, and the truth will set you free."* We can be sure that the more truth we sow into our lives, the greater the harvest of freedom we will reap.

I love how Rick Warren puts it: *"You can build your life on truth, or you can build your life on trends. You want to be hip? You want to be in style and up to date? Fine. But if you build your life on what other people think, what happens when they change their opinion and, all the sudden, what once was so trendy is now out of style? The only way to be externally relevant is to build your life on eternal truths that don't change."*

Truth does not change. It transcends ALL things; age, race, generation, circumstances, economic status, celebrity, education, etc. The truth in God's word will never die or grow old and out of date. It is alive and continues to be the same through every generation past and every generation to come. When we plant this truth in our life we have a guarantee! That guarantee is that His truth planted in our life will not produce nothing! How do we know that? Remember that He promises in Isaiah 55:10–11 that His word will not return to Him empty because it is planted with purpose and it *will* produce a plentiful harvest in our lives, in season.

In Hebrews 4:12 (NIV) it says, *"The word of God is alive and active. Sharper than any double-edged sword, it penetrates even to dividing soul and spirit, joints and marrow; it judges the thoughts and attitudes of the heart."*

I love the phrase "*alive and active*" because it accurately shows the Bible to be an active force in our life. It's like the classic Star Wars phrase, *"May the force be with you!"* The truth is the force is with you and within you! In fact the Greek meaning of this phrase is *"having vital power in itself and exerting the same upon the soul."* God wants His vital power to come from within your spirit and exert truth on your soul.

Let's take a minute and talk about this briefly. *Remember in the beginning week we talked about the difference between your soul, spirit, and body?* The Word of God is the only force with the ability to divide these things perfectly. The Word sifts through our soul issues and weaknesses. It then brings to life our spirit's identity, reminding us who we are meant to be.

This is why having your own life in the Word is vital. It's impossible for someone to know what's going on inside of you. Only God knows what's in your heart. Only He has the ability to help you understand what your heart is saying. A life in the Word is never wasted! The more seeds of truth you can get into your soil, the more you will harvest vital power in your life and reap freedom. *That's the abundant, vibrant life!*

(M) MORNING MEDITATION

"How shall a young man cleanse his way? By taking heed and keeping watch [on himself] according to Your word [conforming his life to it]." Psalm 119:9 (AMP)

How have you actively tried to conform your life to God's Word?

Reading and studying his word. Applying his word to my identity and situations and trying to remember his word throughout the day

(D) DAYTIME DARE

How much time do you spend watching TV or looking at the Internet each week?

How much time do you spend in God's word each week?

Does this ratio show you what you are most interested in learning about?

Use some of your TV or Internet time today to read the Bible. Write down the benefits you felt from doing this.

helps me to feel closer to him even when I am just relaxing

EVENING REFLECTION

I think the Psalmist said it well, *"Remember what you said to me, your servant— I hang on to these words for dear life! These words hold me up in bad times; yes, your promises rejuvenate me. The insolent ridicule me without mercy, but I don't budge from your revelation. I watch for your ancient landmark words, and know I'm on the right track. But when I see the wicked ignore your directions, I'm beside myself with anger. I set your instructions to music and sing them as I walk this pilgrim way. I meditate on your name all night, God, treasuring your revelation, O God. Still, I walk through a rain of derision because I live by your Word and counsel."* Psalm 119:9 (MSG)

Meditate on this. What stays with you?

That his word will hold me up and give me solid ground. It is my armour. He is to be my focus at all times and my constant instructor

"Tears are only seeds if you have hope."
—*Bill Johnson*

Researchers found that the most joyful Christians have four specific characteristics:

1. A feeling of being forgiven
2. Forgiving others
3. A feeling of life purpose
4. A strong sense of gratitude

Let's take a look at each of these characteristics more closely so that we can allow the seeds of joy to grow deep in our soil.

1. **A Feeling of Being Forgiven**

   When we know our sins have been wiped clean and our past is completely forgiven, we have joy. Psalms 51 links joy and salvation together. It says, *"Restore to me the joy of my salvation."* Joy and salvation are twins! You can't have one without the other. We lack joy when we no longer see ourselves as completely forgiven and the cross is not equal to all people. When we understand we have all been given a fair chance at grace, joy is built. Once we understand forgiveness is an equal opportunity we can then give it to others. This leads us to our second point...

2. **Forgiving Others**

   It's impossible to give something away to someone else without first having possessed it ourselves. If we want to love others well, we have to love ourselves well. You cannot give away what you do not have! When we have a hard time forgiving others it's usually linked to our ability to receive forgiveness for ourselves. If we don't believe we are fully forgiven, we have no joy, and we will find it hard to forgive others. It's hard to be joyful when we have unforgiveness in our hearts.

It's a whole lot easier to forgive others when we understand that it truly benefits us the most. When we understand the purpose of forgiveness we will be more prone to give it away. Which leads us to our third point...

3. **A Feeling of Life Purpose**

Joy is directly linked to accomplishment. When we accomplish what we set out to do, we experience deep satisfaction. When we live the life we were created to live, we will experience joy! If you lack joy, you usually lack purpose. But purpose looks different in the Kingdom of Heaven. It's not what we have, who we know, or who knows us, but rather it is an ability to see our life from heaven's perspective and agree (or align ourselves) with that perspective.

The best way to develop joy is to develop purpose. When we understand our purpose, personally and corporately, we know where we are going. It gives us vision and parameters on how to live our life. It gives us balance. The Bible says, *"Find out what pleases God and do it."* Once we know what pleases God, we can do it well. It produces joy!

In Day 23 we likened gratitude to a filter through which we see our lives. Gratitude is linked directly to joy. It's the fourth catalyst to joy: A Strong Sense of Gratitude.

MORNING MEDITATION

We now know how to grow joy but do we know what kills joy?
Burnout! Burnout is described as *"mental or emotional ex-*
haustion," but it can have physical elements as well, like head-
aches or lack of energy. It's often a result of life being too
demanding. Researchers have found burnout to be a natural
result of excessive interpersonal conflicts, dealing with other
people's problems all day, or receiving fewer rewards or affir-
mation from one's accomplishments. This is why it is vital that
we understand what God is calling us to do in our lives! He
is the only one that can keep us from burnout. But we must
purpose to obey *only* what He is asking us to do, not what
others may be pressuring us to do (or what we might be
pressuring ourselves to do because of the need we see). Is
there an area in your life where you are feeling burned out?
What is God asking you to do and not to do? Spend some
time asking Him and write down what He says.

School, relationships - push through
it and he will lead me where
I am meant to go and
is taking care of me along
the way

DAYTIME DARE

Today you have an opportunity to practice joy! Joy is something we can apply to all situations. So, take one mundane
task that you regularly do throughout your day. Actively
commit to do this mundane task with an attitude of joy.
Purpose in your heart to finish well!

"Those who sow with tears will reap with songs of joy."
Psalm 126:5 (NIV)

This verse has deeper meaning than at first glance. The Bible is telling us that we may "sow" tears on earth, but eventually we will "reap" joy; if not here and now on our earth, then without doubt, we will experience joy in our heavenly home.

I love the quote, *"Relying on yourself and your own strength is the opposite of sowing in tears."* (Bill Johnson) It's our ability to choose dependency on God in the struggle that will eventually mean that we reap joy in our lives. Psalm 126:4–6 in The Message Bible says this so well...

"And now, God, do it again— bring rains to our drought-stricken lives. So those who planted their crops in despair will shout hurrahs at the harvest. So those who went off with heavy hearts will come home laughing, with armloads of blessing."

Take a moment to write down anything God is speaking to you about today:

he will get me through
he will take me to a
place where I can rest
forever

FINAL THOUGHTS

Throughout the Bible we see foundational truths hidden in the text.

The Word of God is like a 3-D picture. It's difficult to see the entire scene without looking at it further.

Do you remember those pictures that have 3-D images hidden in them? I remember walking past them in store windows. There would be a small group of people gathered around them staring intently at what looked like a simple image. But every once in a while you would hear someone quietly say, *"I see it!"* They would then walk off with a smile on their face celebrating their small victory. There was nothing more frustrating than standing there as others came and left, still trying to see what everyone else saw.

The Bible is like this image. You have to take time to look at it over and over again, adjusting your gaze; looking for the hidden treasure not easily seen. Once you see it, it's hard to miss. *Have faith, you'll get this!*

Growing a vibrant life requires seeing the big picture. It's about standing back and acknowledging the process we must take. Courageously seeing our ability for radical growth through daily discipline, practical application, and a tender heart will make a huge difference.

Don't be afraid to start small. Don't be afraid to give God your mustard seed. We must see that in God's story, many things began small but grew into larger things.

Moses' courageous journey to leave Egypt led him to the Promised Land. Noah built an ark. And by faith, Jonah finally made it to Nineveh and gave the word of the Lord, which turned an entire people back to God. Esther prepared for six months to present herself to the king, then won his heart and saved an entire nation. Jesus spent thirty years of His life preparing for three years of ministry! (See Hebrews 13)

It's in the law of sowing and reaping that we begin to experience substantial growth in our lives. The ability to lean into this principle allows us to multiply what we have been given, no matter how small. God is not afraid of the smallness of our starting point! He's confident that with our faith, as small as a mustard seed, we will move mountains.

Do you remember the last Law of Growth we talked about in the introduction of this book?

Progressing through all stages of development can only be considered successful growth.

There are NO short cuts when it comes to full maturity. We may make it to our promised land sooner than 40 years, but we all have to walk through the desert. Maturity isn't a gift... it's a process. Have faith. *You may not be where you want to be but...You're on your way!*

Like you, I have dreams yet to be fulfilled. I'm still sowing seeds everyday and there are more things I want to experience in God. I still want to continue to live a vibrant life, pursuing consistent growth in every season I find myself in. Life is not so much about the place of arrival but the journey of destiny.

So, my friend, keep up the good work! Continue to live a life worthy of the call (see Ephesians 4:1) for the One who is worthy of it all. If you live your life to honor Him, He will honor you!

ABOUT HAVILAH

I always knew God had a plan for other's lives, but never felt God could use me. I struggled with learning disabilities throughout my school years, which caused me to have great insecurity about my value and worth. It wasn't until the age of 17, as I was sitting in a car with friends on my way to a party, when I heard the voice of God speak to my heart, "There is more to life than this! I have called you. Come follow me." I spoke out in that moment, telling those in the car that I had a call on my life and they were welcome to come with me, but I was going to serve God.

I remember walking into our house when I got home, kneeling by my bed and saying these simple words, "God, I'm not much. I'm young, I'm a girl with no special gifting. But if You can use anyone, You can use me." Now, thinking back to that day, it makes me laugh how I'd hoped the heavens would have opened up, with angels descending and ascending on a heavenly ladder – that didn't happen and I didn't need it to. God heard my cry and He was at work to accomplish His perfect will in my life.

By 19, my twin sister Deborah and I were traveling all over California preaching, teaching and singing at any place that would have us. By 21, we had been in seven different states and Mexico teaching about Jesus and His great plan for this generation!

I believe today is the Church's finest hour, if we choose to live with passion, purpose and walk in power. I'm passionate about seeing individuals encounter God in a real way and seek to blow the lid off common misconceptions, personal limitations and powerless living. My heart and passion is to inspire and challenge others to become all God has designed them to be.

Havilah

HAVILAH'S RESOURCES

STUDIES / DEVOTIONALS

Keep Calm & Finsih Strong   I Do Hard Things   Radical Growth

TEACHINGS

Becoming a Voice   Free Your Mind   Annointed & Qualified

Find these and other great resources at havilahcunnington.com

STAY CONNECTED

website   *havilahcunnington.com*

facebook   *Havilah Cunnington*

twitter   *@mrshavilah*

instagram   *havilahcunnington*

youtube   *youtube.com/user/havilahcunnington*

email   *info@havilahcunnington.com*

FOR MORE INFORMATION
email info@havilahcunnington.com

join our newsletter

REQUEST HAVILAH TO SPEAK

WOMEN **+** STUDENTS **+** CHURCHES

FOR
*Retreats, conferences, one-night gatherings,
church services, leadership events*

Made in the USA
San Bernardino, CA
19 September 2014